GRATEFUL TO LIFE & DEATH

GRATEFUL
TO LIFE & DEATH

By

R. K. NARAYAN

The Michigan State College Press

1953

Dedicated

to

My Wife

RAJAM

Manufactured in the United States of America
by The Haddon Craftsmen, Inc., Scranton, Pa.

CHAPTER ONE

I WAS on the whole very pleased with my day—not many conflicts and worries, above all not too much self-criticism. I had done almost all the things I wanted to do, and as a result I felt heroic and satisfied. The urge had been upon me for some days past to take myself in hand. What was wrong with me? I couldn't say, some sort of vague disaffection, a self-rebellion I might call it. The feeling again and again came upon me that as I was nearing thirty I should cease to live like a cow (perhaps, a cow, with justice, might feel hurt at the comparison), eating, working in a manner of speaking, walking, talking, etc.—all done to perfection, I was sure, but always leaving behind a sense of something missing.

I took stock of my daily life. I got up at eight every day, read for the fiftieth time Milton, Carlyle and Shakespeare, looked through compositions, swallowed a meal, dressed, and rushed out of the hostel just when the second bell sounded at college; four hours later I returned to my room; my duty in the interval had been admonishing, cajoling and brow-beating a few hundred boys of Albert Mission College so that they might mug up Shakespeare and Milton and secure high marks and save me adverse remarks from my chiefs at the end of the year. For this pain the authorities kindly paid me a hundred rupees on the first of every month and dubbed me a lecturer. One ought, of course, to be thankful and rest content. But such repose was not in my nature, perhaps because I was a poet, and I was constantly nagged by the feeling that I was doing the wrong work. This was responsible for a perpetual self-criticism and all kinds of things aggravated it.

For instance what my good chief Brown had said to us that day might be very reasonable, but it irritated and upset me.

We were summoned to his room at the end of the day. Under normal conditions, he would welcome us with a smile, crack a joke or two, talk of nothing in particular for a couple of minutes and then state the actual business. But to-day we found him dry and sullen. He motioned us to our seats and said, "Could you imagine a worse shock for me? I came across a student of the English Honours, who did not know till this day that 'honours' had to be spelt with a 'u'?" He finished his sentence with a sharp, grim laugh. We looked at each other and were at a loss to know what to reply. Our Assistant Professor, Gajapathy, scowled at us as if it were us who had induced the boy to drop the 'u'. Brown cleared his throat as a signal for further speech, and we watched his lips. He began a lecture on the importance of the English language, and the need for preserving its purity. Brown's thirty years in India had not been ill-spent if they had opened the eyes of Indians to the need for speaking and writing correct English! The responsibility of the English department was indeed very great. At this point Gajapathy threw us a further furious look. The chief went on for forty-five minutes; and feeling that it was time to leaven his sermon with a little humour, added: "It would be a serious enough blunder even from a mathematics honours man!"

When going out I was next to Gajapathy. He looked so heavily concerned that I felt like pricking him so that he might vanish like a bubble leaving no trace behind. But I checked myself. It would be unwise: he was my senior in office, and he might give me an hour of extra work every day, or compel me to teach the history of language, of which I knew nothing. I had to bear with him till we reached the hostel gate. He kept glancing at his own shoulder, swelling with importance. He muttered: "Disgraceful! I never knew our boys were so bad. . . . We cannot pretend that we come out of it with flying colours. . . ." I felt irritated and said, "Mr.

Gajapathy, there are blacker sins in this world than a dropped vowel." He stopped on the road and looked up and down. He was aghast. I didn't care. I drove home the point: "Let us be fair. Ask Mr. Brown if he can say in any of the two hundred Indian languages: 'The cat chases the rat'. He has spent thirty years in India."

"It is all irrelevant," said Gajapathy.

"Why should he think the responsibility for learning is all on our side and none on his? Why does he magnify his own importance?"

"Good night," said Gajapathy and was off. I felt angry and insulted, and continued my discussion long after both Gajapathy and Brown were out of my reach. Later when I went for a walk I still continued the debate. But suddenly I saw illumination and checked myself. It showed a weak, uncontrolled mind, this incapacity to switch off. I now subjected myself to a remorseless self-analysis. Why had I become incapable of controlling my own thoughts? I brooded over it. Needless to say it took me nowhere. It left me more exhausted and miserable at the end of the day. I felt a great regret at having spent a fine evening in brooding and self-analysis, and then reached a startlingly simple solution. All this trouble was due to lack of exercise and irregular habits: so forthwith I resolved to be up very early next day, go out along the river on a long walk, run a few yards, bathe in the river and regulate my life thus.

§

After dinner my friends in the neighbouring rooms in the hostel dropped in as usual for light talk. They were my colleagues. One was Rangappa who taught the boys philosophy, and the other Gopal of the mathematics section. Gopal was sharp as a knife-edge where mathematical matters were concerned, but, poor fellow, he was very dumb and stupid in other matters. As a matter of fact he paid little attention to anything else. We liked him because he was a genius, and

(3)

in a vague manner we understood that he was doing brilliant things in mathematics. Some day he hoped to contribute a paper on his subject which was going to revolutionize human thought and conceptions. But God knew what it was all about. All that I cared for in him was that he was an agreeable friend, who never contradicted and who patiently listened for hours, though without showing any sign of understanding.

To-night the talk was all about English spelling and the conference we had with Brown. I was incensed as usual, much to the amazement of Rangappa. "But my dear fellow, what do you think they pay you for unless it is for dotting the i's and crossing the t's?" Gopal, who had been listening without putting in a word of his own, suddenly became active.

"I don't follow you," he said.

"I said the English department existed solely for dotting the i's and crossing the t's."

"Oh!" he said, opening wide his eyes. "I never thought so. Why should you do it?" His precise literal brain refused to move where it had no concrete facts or figures to grip. Symbols, if they entered his brain at all, entered only as mathematical symbols.

Rangappa answered: "Look here, Gopal. You have come across the expression 'Raining cats and dogs'?"

"Yes."

"Have you actually seen cats and dogs falling down from the sky?"

"No, no. Why?"

Rangappa would have worried him a little longer, but the college clock struck ten and I said: "Friends, I must bid you good night." "Good night," Gopal repeated mechanically and rose to go. Not so the ever-questioning philosopher. "What has come over you?" he asked, without moving.

"I want to cultivate new habits. . . ."

"What's wrong with the present ones?" he asked and I blinked for an answer. It was a long story and could not

(4)

stand narration. Rangappa did not even stir from his seat; the other stood ready to depart and waited patiently. "Answer me," Rangappa persisted.

"I want to be up very early to-morrow," I said.

"What time?"

"Some time before five."

"What for?"

"I want to see the sunrise, and get some exercise before I start work."

"Very good; wake me up too, I shall also go with you—" said Rangappa rising. I saw them off at the door. I had an alarm clock on which I could sometimes depend for giving the alarm at the set time. I had bought it years before at a junk store in Madras. It had a reddening face, and had been oiled and repaired a score of times. It showed the correct time but was eccentric with regard to its alarm arrangement. It let out a shattering amount of noise, and it sometimes went off by itself and butted into a conversation, or sometimes when I had locked the room and gone out, it started off and went on ringing till exhaustion overcame it. There was no way of stopping it, by pressing a button or a lever. I don't know if it had ever had such an arrangement. At first I did not know about its trouble, so that I suffered a great shock and did not know how to silence it, short of dashing it down. But one day I learnt by some sort of instinctive experiment that if I placed a heavy book like Taine's *History of English Literature* on its crest, it stopped shrieking.

I picked up the clock and sat on my bed looking at it. I believe I almost addressed it: "Much depends upon you." I set it at four-thirty and lay down.

At four-thirty it shrieked my sleep away. I switched on the light, picked up Taine hurriedly, and silenced it. I went over to Rangappa's room, stood at his window and called him a dozen times, but there was no answer. As I stood looking at his sleeping figure with considerable disgust and pity, he stirred and asked: "Who is there?"

"It is nearing five, you wanted to be called out—"

"Why?"

"You said you would come out."

"Not me—"

"It is about five—" I said.

"It looks to me like midnight; go back to bed my dear fellow, don't hang about windows pestering people—" His voice was thick and the last words trailed off into sleep.

I stepped out of the hostel gates. Our college and hostel were not more than a couple of hundred yards from the river. There was a narrow lane to be crossed and at the end of it we were on the sands. As I walked down the lane a couple of municipal lamps were still burning, already showing signs of paling before the coming dawn. The eastern skyline was reddening, and I felt triumphant. I could not understand how people could remain in bed when there was such a glory awaiting them outside. I thought of Rangappa. "A dry philosopher I suppose—not susceptible to these influences. A hopeless man. In any case not my business. . . ."

The sand was damp with the morning dew, but as I buried my feet, they felt deep down the warmth of the previous day's sun. In the half-dark dawn I saw some persons already out at work, fording the river, bathing and washing. There were immense banyan trees hanging over the river, and birds stirred and chirped in their nests. I walked on at an even pace, filling my lungs with morning air, and taking great strides. I felt I was really in a new world. I walked nearly four miles down the bank. Before turning back, I selected a clean spot, undressed, and plunged into the water. Coming on shore and rubbing myself with the towel, I felt I had a new lease of life. No doubt in my village home and in this very river I had often bathed, but at no other time could I remember such a glow of joy as filled me now. How could I account for it? There was something in the deliberate effort, and the hour and the air, and surroundings. . . . Nature, nature, all our poets repeat till they are hoarse. There are subtle, invisible emanations in nature's surroundings: with them the deepest in us merges and harmonizes. I think it is the highest form of joy and peace we can ever comprehend. I decided to rush back to my table and write a poem on nature.

I was going to write of the cold water's touch on the skin, the cold air blowing on chest and face, the rumble of the river, cries of birds, magic of the morning light, all of which created an alchemy of inexplicable joy. I paused for a moment and wondered how this poem would be received in a class-room—the grim tolerance with which boys listen to poetry, the annotator's desperate effort to convey a meaning, and the teacher's doubly desperate effort to wrest a meaning out of the poet and the annotator, the essence of an experience lost in all this handling. . . .

I returned to my room before seven. I felt very well satisfied indeed with my performance. I told myself: "I am all right. I am quite sound if I can do this every day. I shall be able to write a hundred lines of poetry, read everything I want to read, in addition to class-work. . . ." This gave place to a distinct memory of half a dozen similar resolves in the past and the lapses . . . I checked this defeatism! "Don't you see this is entirely different? I am different to-day . . ."

"How?" asked a voice. I ignored the question and it added, "Why?"

"Shut up," I cried. "Don't ask questions." I myself was not clear as to the "Why?", except that my conscience perpetually nagged over arrears of work, books from libraries and friends lying in a heap on the table untouched, letters unanswered and accumulating, lines of poetry waiting for months to be put on paper, a picture of my wife meant to be framed and hung on the wall, but for months and months standing on the table leaning against the wall in its cardboard mount, covered with dust, bent by the weight of the books butting into it. . . .

This table assailed my sight as soon as I entered and I muttered "Must set all this right", as I sat down on my chair.

I called Singaram our servant. He had been a hostel servant for forty years and known all of us as undergraduates and now as teachers—an old man who affected great contempt for all of us, including our senior professors and principal. He spoke to us with habitual rudeness. Somehow he felt that because he had seen all of us as boys, our present stature and age and position were a make-believe, to which he would be no party. "Singaram," I called, and he answered from somewhere, "You will have to wait till I come. If you hurt your throat calling me, don't hold me responsible for it. . . ." In a few minutes he stood before me, a shrunken old fellow, with angry wrinkles on his face. "Now what is it this time? Has that sweeper not done her work properly? If she is up to her old tricks . . ."

"Tell the cook to bring my coffee. . . ."

"So late! Why should you dally over your coffee so long, when you ought to be reading at your table? . . ."

"I went for a bathe in the river, Singaram. I found it very fine. . . ." He was happy to hear it.

"I'm glad you are ceasing to be the sort who lounges before bathrooms, waiting for a hot bath. A river bath is the real thing for a real man. I am eighty years old, and have never had a day's sickness, and have never bathed in hot water."

"Nor in cold water, I think," I said as he went away to send me my coffee.

I made a space on the table by pushing aside all the books; took out a sheet of paper and wrote a poem entitled "Nature", about fifty lines of verse. I read and re-read it, and found it very satisfying. I felt I had discharged a duty assigned to me in some eternal scheme.

I had four hours of teaching to do that day. *Lear* for the Junior B.A. class, a composition period for the Senior Arts; detailed prose and poetry for other classes. Four periods of continuous work and I hadn't prepared even a page of lecture.

I went five minutes late to the class, and I could dawdle

over the attendance for a quarter of an hour. I picked out the attendance register and called out the first name.

"Here, sir—", "Present", and I marked. Two boys in the front bench got up and suggested "Sir, take the attendance at the end of the period."

"Sit down please, can't be done. I can't encroach into the next hour's work. . . ."

A babble rose in the class, a section demanding that the attendance be taken immediately and another demanding postponement. I banged the table with my fist and shouted over the din: "Stop this, otherwise I will mark everyone absent."

"Attendance takes up most of our hours, sir."

"We can't help it. Your attendance is just as important as anything else. Stop all noise and answer your names; otherwise, I will mark all of you absent. . . ." At this the boys became quiet, because I out-shouted them. The lion-tamer's touch! In a sober moment perhaps I would reflect on the question of obedience. Born in different households, perhaps petted, pampered, and bullied, by parents, uncles, brothers—all persons known to them and responsible for their growth and welfare. Who was I that they should obey my command? What tie was there between me and them? Did I absorb their personalities as did the old masters and merge them in mine? I was merely a man who had mugged earlier than they the introduction and the notes in the Verity edition of *Lear*, and guided them through the mazes of Elizabethan English. I did not do it out of love for them or for Shakespeare but only out of love for myself. If they paid me the same one hundred rupees for stringing beads together or tearing up paper bits every day for a few hours, I would perhaps be doing it with equal fervour. But such reflections do not mar our peace when we occupy the class-room chair. So that I banged the table—shouted till they were silenced, and went through the attendance; all this tittle-tattle swallowed up half an hour.

I opened my Verity. I had made a pencil mark where I

(9)

had stopped on the previous day: middle of the first scene in the third act.

I began in a general way: "You will see that I stopped last time where Lear faces the storm. This is a vital portion of this great tragedy. . . ." The words rang hollow in my ears. Some part of me was saying: "These poor boys are now all attention, cowed by your superior force. They are ready to listen to you and write down whatever you may say. What have you to give them in return?" I noticed that some boys were already sitting up alert, ready to note down the pearls dropping from my mouth. . . . I felt like breaking out into a confession! "My dear fellows, don't trust me so much. I ám merely trying to mark time because I couldn't come sufficiently prepared, because all the morning I have . . ." But I caught myself lecturing: "This is the very heart of the tragedy and I would like you to follow this portion with the greatest attention. . . ." I stole a look at the watch. . . . Only fifteen minutes more. "As usual I shall read through this scene first, and then I shall take it up in detail. . . ." I looked at the page on the table—"Enter Lear and Fool. Blow winds and crack your cheeks! Rage! Blow! You cataracts and hurricanes, spout till you have drenched our steeples, drowned the cocks! . . ." As I read on I myself was moved by the force and fury of the storm compressed in these lines. The sheer poetry of it carried me on. . . .

". . . And thou, all-shaking Thunder
    Strike flat the thick rotundity o' the world!"
I forgot all about the time, all about my unpreparedness.

". . . Let the great gods
    That keep this dreadful pother o'er our heads,
    Find out their enemies now."
I read on. The boys listened attentively. I passed on to the next scene without knowing it. I could not stop.

"Poor naked wretches, wheresoe'er you are,
    That hide the pelting of this pitiless storm,

How shall your houseless heads and unfed sides,
. . . defend you
From seasons such as these?"
At the thought of helpless humanity I nearly broke down.
The bell rang, I shut my book with the greatest relief, and
walked out of the class.

I managed the composition hour quite easily. The composition hour is a sort of relaxation for us, where we can sit
looking at notebooks and do not demand too much attention
from the boys. It was the small gallery room at the end of
the southern corridor; I loved this room because the sun
came through a ventilator, bringing in a very bright beam
of light, and brilliant dust particles floated in it, and the two
boys who sat on the second bench looked all aflame. Years
and years ago I sat there on the bench as a student, and
Gajapathy was then just a junior lecturer and not the big
Assistant Professor he was now. I could still see where I used
to sit assiduously cultivating correct language and trying to
please the lecturer. And to my left would always sit Rangappa, who hated all composition. Little did I dream then
that I would be a teacher in the same class.

The boys were making too much noise. I tapped the table
lightly and said: "Ramaswami, here is your notebook. See the
corrections on it. There are more corrections on it than on
any other paper. . . ." It was a paraphrase of the poem
beginning "My days among the dead are past . . ." He
hadn't understood a line of that poem, yet he had written
down two pages about it. According to Ramaswami (though
not according to Southey) the scholar when he said, "My
days among the dead are past" meant that he was no longer
going to worry about his dead relations because wherever
his eyes were cast he saw mighty minds of old (he just copies
it down from the poem), and so on and on. I enjoyed this
paraphrase immensely. I called, "Ramaswami, come and receive your notebook. . . ." My comments on the work could

(11)

not be publicly shown or uttered. When he came near, I opened the notebook and pointed to my remark at the end of the notebook: "Startling!" I put my finger on this and asked: "Do you see what I mean?"

"Yes, sir . . ." whispered Ramaswami.

"You are very bad in English."

"I am sorry, sir. . . ."

"Does this poem make no sense as far as you are concerned?"

"No, sir. . . ."

"Then why do you write so much about it?"

"I do not know, sir. . . ."

"All right, go back to your seat. . . . Come and see me sometime. . . ."

"Yes, sir, when?"

I couldn't answer this question, because I visualized all my hours so thoroughly allotted for set tasks that I was at a loss to know when I could ask him to see me. So I replied: "I will tell you, go to your seat." I spent the rest of the period giving a general analysis of the mistakes I had encountered in this batch of composition—*rather very, as such* for *hence*, split infinitives, collective nouns, and all the rest of the traps that the English language sets for foreigners. I then set them an exercise in essay-writing on the epigram "Man is the master of his own destiny." "An idiotic theme," I felt, "this abstract and confounded metaphysic;" but I could not help it. I had been ordered to set this subject to the class. I watched with interest how the boys were going to tackle it. As a guidance it was my duty to puff up this theme, and so I wrote on the blackboard—"Man, what is man? What is destiny? How does he overcome destiny? How does destiny overcome him? What is fate? What is free will?"—a number of headings which reduced man and his destiny and all the rest to a working formula for these tender creatures to handle.

By the afternoon I had finished three hours of lecturing,

and was, with a faintly smarting throat, resting in a chair in the common room. There were a dozen other teachers. As each of them sat looking at a book or at the ceiling vacantly, there was a silence which seemed to me oppressive. I never liked it. I had my own technique of breaking it. I remarked to no one in particular: "We have to decide an important issue before the examinations begin." The others looked up with bored half-expectancy. "We will have to call a staff meeting to decide how many marks are to be deducted for spelling honours with the middle u."

"No, no, I don't think it is necessary," said Sastri, the logic lecturer, who had a very straightforward, literal mind, looking up for a moment from the four-day old newspaper which he was reading. Gajapathy looked over his spectacles, and remarked from the farthest end of the room: "You are joking over yesterday's meeting, I suppose?" I replied, "I am not joking, I am very serious."

"What is it all about?" Dr. Menon asked. He was Assistant Professor of Philosophy. Gajapathy explained, slowly, like an expert lawyer, what had happened the previous evening.

"No sense of proportion . . ." was the philosopher's verdict. Gajapathy removed his spectacles, folded the sides, and put them away as a preparation for dispute. "How would you treat one of your students if he spelt *Kant, Cant?*"

"I wouldn't bother very much if he knew correctly what Kant had or hadn't said," replied Dr. Menon.

"Oh, I won't believe it," said Gajapathy, "there is a merit in accuracy, which must be cultivated for its own sake. I believe it wouldn't do to slacken anywhere."

"Americans spell honours without the u," I said and this diverted the subject, and deprived Gajapathy of the duel for which he was preparing. "Americans are saner than their English cousins in most matters," said Dr. Menon, who had obtained his Ph.D., at Columbia University.

(13)

"I think the American spelling is foolish buffoonery," said Gajapathy with his loyalty of a life-time to English language and literature.

"If we had Americans ruling us, I suppose we would say the same thing of the English people," I said.

"Politics need not butt in everywhere. There are times when I wish there were no politics in the world and no one knew who was ruling and how," said Gajapathy. "This would help a little clearer, freer thinking in all matters. The whole of the West is in a muddle owing to its political consciousness, and what a pity that the East should also follow suit. It is like a weed choking all other human faculties. Shelley in his 'Sensitive Plant' . . ."

"I am afraid your opinions are at least a thousand years behind the times; it is a one-sided view, Mr. Gajapathy," said Kumar, who lectured on political science to B.A. classes. "Corporate life marks the beginning of civilized existence and the emergence of its values. . . ."

"I am sure," I said, finding the debate dull, "a tormenting question can be framed for the boys at the next examination. 'Corporate existence pulled the cave man out into the open. Discuss.' If I have anything to do with the politics paper I'm going to insist on this question and make it compulsory. It will serve the young rascals right. . . ."

"You haven't yet dropped the frivolous habits of your college days, Krishna," said Gajapathy. "You must cultivate a little more seriousness of outlook."

"I have answered an advertisement I saw in an American paper where someone has offered to take on hand people who lack seriousness and turn them into better citizens. I have filled up the necessary coupon and have every hope you will find me passable ere long. . . ."

"Don't you believe too much in these ads. In the United States there are any number of them. Once when I was in Chicago . . ." began Dr. Menon of Columbia University, and the bell rang and all his audience rose to go to their different classes.

§

I returned to my room. The postman had slipped through the door two letters for me. I knew the pale blue envelope from my wife, who was in the habit of underlining the town three times; she seemed to be always anxious lest the letter should go off to some other town. And then my father's letter, from the village. Letters are very exciting things for me. I don't know why. By the time I open and see the contents, I feel an æon might have passed, and my heart goes thumping against my ribs. I looked through my father's letter first. He still wrote his fine, sharp hand, every letter put down with precision and care but without ornament, written closely on a memo pad of some revenue department. From time immemorial he had written only on those pads. No one knew how many pads he had or how he had come by them—perhaps through the favour of some friend in the Revenue Department. The paper had acquired an elegant tone of brown through years of storing but it was tough as parchment. My father had a steel pen with a fat green wooden handle, with which he had written for years. He had several bottles of ink —his own make from a recipe which was exclusively his and of which he was excessively proud. He would make up his store of ink once a year; and we little ones of the household waited for the event with tremendous enthusiasm—all the servants in the house would be present: a special brick oven was raised in the backyard, with a cauldron sizzling over it all day, and father presiding. The most interesting part, however, would be the trip the previous evening for shopping to Kavadi—our nearest town, fifteen miles off. At three in the afternoon father would yoke the big bulls to the waggon and we were dressed and ready for the expedition—I and my elder brother, and my two sisters. My elder brother would exact obedience and we would have to take our seats in the cart according to his directions. The way he handled us we always expected he would become a commander of an army or a police officer—but the poor fellow settled as auditor in Hyderabad and was nose-led by his wife. He was always full of worries, being a father of ten, and having a haughty nagging wife. He seldom visited us in the village being so much wrapped up in his own auditing and family.

We reached Kavadi at about two o'clock. Invariably I would fall to sleep lulled by the jingling of the bells around the necks of the bulls.

Kavadi was a wonderful place for one like me from the village—a street full of all sorts of shops, sewing machines rattling away, coloured ribbons streaming down from shopfronts. My father had his favourite shop. The shopman would seat us all on the mat; and my father would buy us some edibles from the opposite shop, while the ink-ingredients were being packed. He would buy us each a toy—a ball, a monkey dangling at the end of a rubber-piece, and a doll, and invariably an exercise book and a pencil for my elder brother, declaring that he was past the age of having toys, a reminder which made him smart every time he heard it. The road would be ankle deep in bleached dust and the numerous cattle and country carts passing along stirred it up so much that a cloud always hung over the road, imparting an enchanting haze to the whole place, though, by the time we started back, so much of this dust settled on our skins and hair that our mother had to give us a bath as soon as we reached home.

I don't know why my father took this ink business so very seriously, when we could buy all the ink we wanted in the shop and save ourselves all bother. He would be near his brick kiln the whole of the next day boiling up this potion, and distilling, and straining, and filling up huge mud jugs. He filled small glass pots for our use, and locked up the store in an *almirah*. We wrote our copies and lessons in this ink. It had a greenish tint which we didn't like, and which made us long for the blue or black ink sold in the shop. We never got over the feeling that this ink was not real ink—perhaps because of its pale greenish tinge, but my father seemed to appreciate it for that very reason declaring that you couldn't buy that elegant shade even if you paid a fortune for it.

My father's letter brought back to me not only the air of the village and all my childhood, but along with it all the facts—home, coconut-garden, harvest, revenue demand. He had devoted nearly a paragraph to my mother's health with a faint suggestion of complaint that she was not looking after herself quite properly—still keeping late hours for food—the last to eat in the house and still reluctant to swallow the medicines given to her. . . .

And then came a paragraph of more immediate interest to me. "Your father-in-law has written a letter to-day. I hear that by God's grace, your wife Susila, and the baby, are keeping well. He suggests that you should take her and the baby and set up a family and not live in a hostel any longer. He has my entire concurrence in this matter, as I think in the best interests of yourself you should.set up a family. You have been in the hostel too long and I don't feel you ought to be wasting the best of your life in the hostel as it will affect your health and outlook. Your mother is also of the same view since your father-in-law's place is not a very healthy one for an infant. If you have no serious objection to this, your father-in-law suggests the 10th of next month as the most suitable and auspicious date . . ."

He was a B.A. of the olden days brought up on Pater and Carlyle and Scott and Browning; personally looked after by Dr. William Miller, Mark Hunter and other eminent professors of Madras College; he was fastidious and precise in handling the English language, though with a very slight pomposity inevitable in the men of those days. After passing his B.A. he refused to enter government service, as many of his generation did, but went back and settled in his village and looked after his lands and property. I said to myself on reading his letter: "God, what am I to do with a little child of seven months? . . ." This somehow seemed to terrify me. How did one manage these things? I had visited my wife's place three or four times since the baby was born. At the first trip I could hardly take notice of the child, although for my wife's sake I had to pinch its cheeks. I no doubt felt a mild affection for it, but there was nothing compelling or indispensable about it. . . . During the subsequent interviews I found more interest in the girl and began to feel that it would be nice to have her about the home, cooing and shouting. . . . But I didn't bargain to accept her guardianship so suddenly. I had seen my sister's children of that age, seven months or eight months old, and they started howling and crying at nights till we felt that they would not survive whatever was afflicting them. But my mother was there, and she could take them in hand expertly: a fomentation, a rub with an oil, some decoction down their throats, and they were quietened.

My father's letter had a postscript: "To help you set up the family your mother is quite willing to come and stay with you for a few weeks. I have not the slightest objection. . . ."

I put down my father's letter. There was much food for thought in it.

I smelt my wife's letter before opening it. It carried with it the fragrance of her trunk, in which she always kept her stationery—a mild jasmine smell surrounded her and all her possessions ever since I had known her. I hurriedly glanced through her letter. In her uniform rotund hand, she had written a good deal about the child which made me want to see her at once. The baby was really too intelligent for her age, understood everything that was being said and done in the house. There was every indication that she was going to prove the most astonishingly intelligent person in the family. She crawled on her belly all over the place, and kept a spy-like watch on her mother's movements. Too cunning! She was learning to say "Appa" (father); and with every look was asking her mother when father proposed to take them home —I liked this, but was not prepared to accept it totally. She then referred to the letter from my father and her father and requested me to set up a house at the earliest moment possible. I felt I was someone whose plans and determinations were of the utmost importance to others. . . .

I placed the letter on the table, locked the room, and went out for a wash. While crossing the quadrangle my eyes fell on a jasmine bush which completely covered our library wall. I had seen it as a very young sapling years and years ago. When I was a student, I had taken a special interest in its growth, and trained it up a small bamboo bower which I had put up with the help of Singaram the old peon. . . . Many persons had laughed at me for it. "Why should we grow a jasmine bush in a boys' hostel?" I was often asked. "Just to remind us that there are better things in the world, that is all," I replied. It was a struggle for existence for that plant, all kinds of cows trespassing into the compound and biting off the stalk. It went up and down several times causing me unending anxiety. And then one day I got the idea of entrusting it to Singaram's care with the suggestion that he might take its flowers, if they appeared, to his womenfolk at home and for the god during the celebration of the Vinayaka festival in the hostel. Since then it grew up under his personal care. He dealt severely with persons who went near it; and as a special favour, occasionally left half a dozen buds on the sill of my window. Now as I passed along to the bathroom I looked at it and said: "I'm about to leave you . . . after all these years . . . after ten years"—the period I had spent in the hostel, first as student and then as teacher. I sighed as I passed it, the only object of any beauty hereabouts. The rest of the quadrangle was mere mud, scorched by Malgudi sun.

I had to wait in the bathroom passage for some time, all the cubicles were engaged. Behind the doors, to the tune of falling water a couple of boys were humming popular film songs. I paced the passage with the towel round my neck. It was a semidark, damp place, with a glass tile giving it its sole lighting. "I shall soon be rid of this nuisance," I reflected, "when I have a home of my own. Hostel bathrooms are hell on earth.

... [God said to his assistants, 'Take this man away to hell', and they brought him down to the hostel bathroom passage, and God said, 'torture him', and they opened the room and pushed him in. . . . No, no, at this moment the angels said 'the room is engaged'. . . . God waited as long as a god can wait and asked 'Have you finished' and they replied 'still engaged', and in due course they could not see where their victim was, for grass had grown and covered him up completely while he waited outside the bathroom door. This promises to be a good poem. Must write it some day . . ."] At this moment a door opened and someone came out dripping. It was a student of the second-year class. He asked agitatedly: "Sir, have I kept you waiting long?"

"Yes, my dear fellow, but how could you come out before finishing that masterpiece of a song?" The other held the door ostentatiously open and I passed in.

I was back in my room. I applied a little hair-cream, stood before the small looking glass hanging by the nail on the wall, and tried to comb. The looking glass was in the southern wall and I could hardly see my face. "Nuisance," I muttered, picked up the glass, and looked for a place to hang it on—not a place. Light at the window struck me in the face and dazzled. "The room is full of windows," I muttered. "These petty annoyances of life will vanish when I have a home of my own. My dear wife will see that the proper light comes at the proper angle." I finally put the looking glass down on the table. It had a stand which would not support it. I picked up Taine's *History of Literature* and leaned the glass against it. "Taine every time," I muttered and combed my hair back, interrupting the operation for a moment to watch the spray from the comb wet-dotting the covers of books and notebooks on the table. I paused for a moment gazing at my face in the glass. "This is how, I suppose, I appear to that girl and the little one. Yet they have confidence that I shall be able to look after them and run a home!"

I was ready to start out. I picked up the letters, smelt once again my wife's epistle, and sat back in the chair, and read

(20)

the letter over again, without missing a single word. "I want to see the baby and her mother very badly. How long am I to be in this wretched hostel?" I said to myself. I leaned back, reflecting. Through my window I could see the college tower and a bit of the sky. I had watched through this window the play of clouds and their mutation for a decade. All that was to be learnt about clouds was learnt by me, sitting in this place, and looking away, while studying for examinations or preparing lectures.

I started out. At the hostel gate I saw Rangappa standing. He was involved in a discussion with Subbaram—an assistant in the Economics Department. I tried to go away pretending not to have seen him.

"Krishna, Krishna! Just a moment," Rangappa cried on seeing me. He turned to his friend and said: "Let us refer it to a third party." I stopped. "You see," began Rangappa. "The point is this . . ."

"No, let me first say what it is," the other interrupted.

"What place would you give to economic values . . ." he began.

"It all depends," I said ironically, without allowing him to finish the sentence.

"No, no, don't put it that way," interrupted Rangappa.

"I will simplify it for you. Is a hundred percent materialism compatible with our best traditions?" Just another of our numerous discussions going on night and day among my colleagues, leading God knew where. What pleasure or profit did they get by it? "I will give the matter deep consideration and tell you in due course," I said, and moved away. Rangappa cried: "Wait, I will go with you."

"I am not going for a walk but to search for a house," I said, and went away.

§

"I must have a house," I told myself, "which faces south, for its breeze, keeps out the western sun, gets in the eastern, and admits the due measure of northern light that artists so

(21)

highly value. The house must have a room for each one of us and for a guest or two. It must keep us all together and yet separate us when we would rather not see each other's faces. . . . We must have helpful people and good people near at hand, but obnoxious neighbours ten miles away. It must be within walking distance of college and yet so far out as to let me enjoy my domestic life free from professional intrusions."

I spent the entire evening scouring various parts of the town watching for "To Let" signs.

"The builder of this house must have been dead-drunk while doing the latter portion of the house. This is a house evidently intended for monkeys to live in. This house must have been designed by a tuberculosis expert so that his business may prosper for the next hundred years. This house is ideal for one whose greatest desire in life is to receive constant knocks on his head from door-posts. A house for a twisted pigmy." Thus, variously, I commented within myself as I inspected the vacant houses in the east, west and south of the town. I scoured South Extension, Fort Area, Racecourse Road, and Vinayak Mudali Street. I omitted Lawley Extension because it was expensive, and also the New Extension beyond it, because it was too far out of the way.

The search extended over three or four days. I could think of nothing but houses all the while. The moment I met anyone I asked: "Can you suggest a good house?" I was becoming a bore, capable of talking of nothing but houses, houses, night and day. I got into the habit of taking aside my students and asking them about it. I was becoming anxious. The day was fast approaching when my wife and child would be arriving. There didn't appear to be a single house fit for their occupation in the whole town. Suppose fifteen days hence I was still in this state and they arrived and had nowhere to go outside the railway station! This vision was a nightmare to me. However I was spared. One of my students knew somebody who knew somebody else who had a house in Sarayu

Street, and who was eager to have a good, cultured family as tenants. "Am I good? Is mine a cultured family?" I asked myself immediately. Sarayu Street was a coveted spot in the town. It fulfilled almost all the conditions that are looked for in a residential locality, cheap houses, refined surroundings, and yet near enough to the market and the offices. I fell into feverish anxiety over this house. The boy promised to take me to the first link in the chain of introductions, on the following morning. I was too impatient to wait till then. I implored him: "There is no sense in postponing these matters. Somebody else may be there before me. Let us go to-day." I visualized the whole town waiting to crowd into the house and fight for it. The boy begged to be let off to-day since his evening was already committed to some other duty, but I brushed aside all his explanations and clung to him fast. He took me to his house behind the market, and then to someone a mile east of the market, and finally to an old man hunched up in a rag-covered cane chair on the veranda of a house in Ellamman Street. It was a very narrow place with the tiles touching one's head, and the chair completely filled the veranda. The old man fussed about on my arrival and compelled me to sit on a stool, which was placed on the edge of the veranda, and I was in constant danger of being tipped off into the street if I moved my limbs a little carelessly. So I sat there holding my breath. He was a very shrunken palsied patriarch. His sight was dim. He strained his eyes to catch a glimpse of me, but did not succeed. A silence fell between us. I broke it by asking: "Are you the owner of the house?"

"No," he replied, promptly, in his querulous voice. "God is the owner and I am his slave."

"What is the rent?"

"First see the house and tell me if you like it." I felt rather cowed by his authoritarian manner. I ventured: "I can't do anything unless I know something about it. . . ." He shook his head reflectively: "Do you want the garage or not?"

"Has it a garage?" I asked.

"Don't ask all that now," said the old man.

"Unless I know first if it has a garage . . ." I said.

"You want everything to be told first," he snapped with disgust, "before you say anything yourself. Go, go away. I am not prepared to talk to you any more. I don't want to give you my house. I have seen hundreds like you who come and ask questions and vanish out of sight."

"What is the matter with you?" I asked indignantly. He bent close to my face and said: "I am semi-blind. Till three months ago, I could see clearly, but it came on suddenly. And I can't talk without faltering: that's what paralysis has done for me: speaking is a strain to me. Otherwise I am prepared to sit here a whole day and wag my tongue to your heart's content, not caring whether you are a true tenant or a bogus one who comes and pesters me by the score each day. I will send the boy along with the key. See the house and then come and talk to me."

"All right," I said. He called a boy, pressed into his hand a large rusty key and said: "Show this master the bungalow. Show him every cupboard," he commanded. I followed the boy out. On the way I tried to engage him in friendly conversation, but he did not want it. He had his pocket filled with fried nuts, and was ceaselessly transferring them to his mouth. He walked ten yards ahead. "What class are you reading in?" "I won't read," he replied. He tossed the key up and caught it in mid-air. He led me through some maze of lanes and took me to Sarayu Street.

Mine was the last house in a particular row. I liked it at first sight. A small wooden gate, ten yards of garden space, and then four steps up to a gabled veranda. There was a small room opening on the veranda detached from the main house. I went in and threw the window open: "A lovely view of Sarayu Street. When I have nothing else to do," I told myself, "I can watch the goings on of Sarayu Street." This room is evidently built for me, where I can study and write without disturbing the household or being disturbed."

"Why has this been untenanted so long?" I asked the boy, without hoping for a reply as the boy waited for me tossing up the lock and key. But he seemed to have melted towards me; and promptly replied, "Because grandfather refuses to give it."

"When was this last occupied?"

"Fifteen days ago," he said.

"Is that all?" I asked, but he suddenly lapsed into his silent ways once again.

I liked the house very much. It had a central hall, "where all of us can meet," and a small room at one end of the hall. "This must be her room and the child's", I told myself. The kitchen and other portions of the house were very satisfactory. There was a cocoanut tree in the backyard. "When a monkey goes up that tree, I can show it to the child," I said, viewing it from the tiny back veranda.

I went back to the old man and said: "I will take the house. What is the rent?"

"H'm," he reflected, "do you want it with or without a garage?" I studiously avoided asking if it had a garage at all and where. I merely said, with a trembling diplomacy: "What'll be the difference with or without. Suppose I want a garage?"

"Hush!" He made a gesture of utter despair. "I don't like you to brag about all that unnecessarily. Empty talk! Don't pretend you own a car. You have come walking. Even if I'm blind, do you think I can't notice it?"

"Look here," I cried, losing all patience. "If you are letting the house, let it, otherwise don't talk of matters which are not your concern. I'm not here to learn lessons from you. I am myself a teacher: and I teach a thousand boys in that college, mind you!" He was greatly impressed.

"College teacher!" He gave a salute with both hands and said, "I revere college teachers, our *Gurus*. Meritorious deeds in previous births make them gurus in this life. I'm so happy. I only wanted a good, cultured family."

(25)

"Everybody knows how good we are, and how cultured our family is!" I replied haughtily. This had the desired effect. I added: "Don't mistake me for an ordinary person!" I drew myself up proudly. He was tremendously impressed. His face beamed with relief: "Do you know why I want a cultured family?" He whispered as if it were a State secret: "I'm going away to live with my son after letting the house, and I want someone who will send me the rent without fail. . . ."

"Depend upon me," I said. "What shall I have to pay you?"

"Twenty-five on the fifth of every month. It must reach me on that day at Bellary."

"Very well. And what about the garage?" I asked haughtily.

"I'll build you one if you want, but ten rupees extra," he said.

"All right, I will tell you when I need one," I said.

§

Four days later my table and trunk and chair were loaded into a bullock cart, my old room was locked up and the key was handed to Singaram. My hostel friends stood on the veranda and cracked a joke or two. The hostel was a place where people constantly arrived and departed and it was not in anyone's nature there to view these matters pensively. Rangappa and the mathematics man stood on the veranda and said: "Well, good-bye, friend. Good luck. Don't forget us for the house-warming," and laughed. Singaram had been very busy the whole day packing up and loading my things. He had attended on me for ten years—sweeping my room, counselling me and running my errands. He walked behind the creaking cart warning the driver: "When you unload, remove the trunk first and the table last. If I hear that you have broken any leg, I will break your head, remember. . . ." I walked behind the cart. Singaram had come to the border of his domain—the hostel drive, and stopped. He salaamed me and said, "Don't forget our hostel, keep visiting us now and then." He hesitated for a moment and said: "Now permit this old man to go. . . ." It was his hint that the time had come for him to receive his reward. He nearly held out his hand for it. I took out my purse and put a rupee on his palm. He looked at me coldly and said: "Is this all the value you attach to the old man?" "Yes," I replied. "I should have given half that to anyone else. . . ."

"No, no, don't say so. Don't grudge an honest man his payment. I've been your servant for ten years. Do you know what Professor X gave me when he left this hostel?" "I don't want all that information," I said and added a nickel to the rupee. He said: "Don't grudge an old servant his due. You will perhaps not see me again: I will perhaps be dead; next year I'm retiring and going back to my village. You will never see me again. You will be very sorry when you hear that old Singaram is dead and that you wouldn't give the poor fellow eight annas more. . . ." I put in his hand an eight-anna coin. He bowed and said: "God will make you a big professor one day. . . ." and walked away. I passed out of the hostel gate, following my caravan and goods.

CHAPTER TWO

THE NEXT three days I was very busy. My table was placed in the front room of the new house. All my papers and books were arranged neatly. My clothes hung on a peg. The rest of the house was swept and cleaned.

My mother arrived from the village with a sack full of vessels, and helped to make up the house for me. She was stocking the store-room and the kitchen and spent most of her time travelling in a *jutka* to the market and coming back with something or other. She worked far into the night, arranging and rearranging the kitchen and the store. At night she sat down with me on the veranda and talked of her house-keeping philosophy. I liked this veranda very much. We had a cool breeze here. I felt immensely satisfied with my choice of the house now. I hoped my wife too would like it. But my mother, the moment she arrived from the village, said, "What an awful kitchen! so narrow! And the dining room would have been better if they had added at least a yard in length that side. . . ."

"We can't have everything our way in a house built by someone else. . . ." I became rather impatient if anyone criticized this house. She understood it and said: "I'm not saying it is a bad house. . . ." She had been used to our large, sprawling home in the village, and everything else seemed to her small and choking. I explained this fact to her and she agreed it was so: "But do you know how hard it is to keep a huge house like ours clean? It takes me a whole lifetime to keep it tidy, but I don't grudge it. Only I want a little more co-operation. Your father is becoming rather difficult nowadays. . . ." She explained how impatient he became when he heard the swish of a broom or the noise of scrubbing, and shouted at her to stop it all. As he was growing old, these noises got on his nerves. And so every time she wanted to clean the house, she had to wait till he went away to the fields. "And do you know, when I delay this, how many other things get out of routine? Unless I have cleaned the house I can't go and bathe. After bathing I've to worship, and only after that can I go near the cows. . . . And if I fail to look at the cowshed for half an hour, do you know what happens?" She was completely wrapped up in her duties. House-keeping was a grand affair for her. The essence of her existence consisted in the thrills and pangs and the satisfaction that she derived in running a well-ordered household. She was unsparing and violent where she met slovenliness. "If a woman can't take charge of a house and run it sensibly, she must be made to get into man's dress and go out in a procession. . . ." I thought of my wife and shuddered at the fate that might be awaiting her in the few weeks my mother was going to stay and help us run the house. My wife was the last daughter of the family and was greatly petted by her parents, in her own house, where she spent most of her time reading, knitting, embroidering or looking after a garden. In spite of it, after my marriage my mother kept her in the village and trained her up in house-keeping. My wife had picked up many sensible points in cooking and household economy, and her own parents were tremendously impressed with her attainments when she next visited them. They were thrilled beyond words and remarked when I went there, "We are so happy, Susila has such a fine house for her training. Every girl on earth should be made to pass through your mother's hands . . ." which, when I conveyed it to my mother, pleased her. She said: "I really do not mind doing it for everyone, but there are those who neither know nor learn when taught. I feel like kicking them when I come across that type." I knew she was referring to her eldest daughter-in-law, my brother's wife, whom she detested heartily. I had half a suspicion that my eldest brother went away to seek his livelihood in Hyderabad solely for this reason, for there used to be very painful scenes at home while the first daughter-in-law was staying in our house, my mother's idiosyncrasy being what it was and the other being of a haughty disposition. She was the daughter of a retired High Court Judge, and would never allow a remark or a look from my mother to pass unchallenged, and as a result great strife existed in the household for a number of years. My mother used to declare when my elder brother was not present, "Whatever happens, even with a ten-thousand rupee dowry, I shall never accept a girl from a High Court Judge's family again. . . ."

It had always been my great anxiety that my wife should not share this fate. My mother seemed to feel that some reference of more immediate interest was due to me and said: "Susila is a modest girl. She is not obstinate." I was grateful for that negative compliment. That was at the beginning of our married years. They had constant contact after that, and with every effort Susila came out better burnished than before. And then came a point when my mother declared: "Susila has learnt how to conduct herself before guests." At this point they separated; now they were meeting again, with Susila having a home of her own to look after, and my mother ready to teach the obedient pupil her business. It was really this which I secretly dreaded.

§

On the following Friday, I was pacing the little Malgudi railway station in great agitation. I had never known such suspense before. She was certain to arrive with a lot of luggage, and the little child. How was all this to be transferred from the train to the platform? and the child must not be hurt. I made a mental note, "Must shout as soon as the train stops: 'Be careful with the baby'." This seemed to my fevered imagination the all-important thing to say on arrival, as otherwise I fancied the child's head was sure to be banged against the doorway. . . . And how many infants were damaged and destroyed by careless mothers in the process of coming out of trains! Why couldn't they make these railway carriages of safer dimensions? It ought to be done in the interests of baby welfare in India. "Mind the baby and the door". And then the luggage! Susila was sure to bring with her a huge amount of luggage. She required four trunks for her sarees alone! Women never understood the importance of travelling light. Why should they? As long as there were men to bear all the anxieties and bother and see them through their travails! It would teach them a lesson to be left to shift for themselves. Then they would know the value of economy in these matters. I wrung my hands in despair. How was she going to get out with the child and all that luggage! The train stopped for just seven minutes. I would help her down first and then throw the things out, and if there were any boxes left over they would have to be lost with the train, that was all. No one could help it. I turned to the gnarled blue-uniformed man behind me. He was known as Number Five and I had known him for several years now. Whatever had to be done on the railway platform was done with his help. I had offered him three times his usual wages to help me to-day. I turned to him and asked: "Can you manage even if there is too much luggage?"

"Yes, master, no difficulty. The train stops for seven minutes." He seemed to have a grand notion of seven minutes; a miserable flash it seemed to me. "We unload whole waggons within that time."

"I will tell the pointsman to stop it at the outer signal, if necessary," he added. It was a very strength-giving statement to me. I felt relieved. But I think I lost my head once again. I believe, in this needless anxiety, I became slightly demented. Otherwise I would not have rushed at the station-master the moment I set eyes on him. I saw him come out of his room and move down the platform to gaze on a far off signal post. I ran behind him, panting: "Good morning stationmaster!" He bestowed an official smile and moved off to the end of the platform and looked up. I felt I had a lot of doubts to clear on railway matters and asked inanely: "Looking at the signals?"

"Yes," he replied, and took his eyes down, and turned to go back to his room. I asked: "Can't they arrange to stop this train a little longer here?" "What for? Isn't there enough trouble as it is?" I laughed sympathetically and said: "I said so because it may not be possible for passengers to unload all their trunks."

"I should like to see a passenger who carries luggage that will take more than six minutes. I have been here thirty years."

I said: "My wife is arriving to-day with the infant. I thought she would require a lot of time in order to get down carefully. And then she is bound to have numerous boxes. These women, you know," I said laughing artificially, seeking his indulgence. He was a good man and laughed with me. "Well, sometimes it has happened that the train was held up for the convenience of a second-class passenger. Are your people travelling second?" "I can't say," I said. I knew well she wouldn't travel second, although I implored her in every letter to do so. She wrote rather diplomatically: "Yes, don't be anxious, I and the baby will travel down quite safely." I even wrote to my father-in-law, but that gentleman preserved a discreet silence on the matter. I knew by temperament he disliked the extravagance of travelling second, although he could afford it and in other ways had proved himself no miser. I felt furious at the thought of him and told the stationmaster: "Some people are born niggards . . . would put up with any trouble rather than . . ." But before I could finish my sentence a bell rang inside the station office and the stationmaster ran in, leaving me to face my travail and anguish alone. I turned and saw my porter standing away from me, borrowing a piece of tobacco from someone. "Here, Number Five, don't get lost." A small crowd was gathering unobtrusively on the platform. I feared he might get lost at the critical moment. A bell sounded. People moved about. We heard the distant puffing and whistling. The engine appeared around the bend.

A whirling blur of faces went past me as the train shot in and stopped. People were clambering up and down. Number Five followed me about, munching his tobacco casually, "Search on that side of the mail van." I hurried through the crowd, peering into the compartments. I saw my father-in-law struggling to get to the doorway. I ran up to his carriage. Through numerous people getting in and out, I saw her sitting serenely in her seat with the baby lying on her lap. "Only three minutes more!" I cried. "Come out!" My father-in-law got down. I and Number Five fought our way up, and in a moment I was beside my wife in the compartment.

"No time to be sitting down; give me the baby," I said. She merely smiled and said: "I will carry the baby down. You will get these boxes. That wicker box, bring it down yourself, it contains baby's bottle and milk vessels." She picked up the child and unconcernedly moved on. She hesitated for a second at the thick of the crowd and said: "Way please," and they made way for her. I cried: "Susila, mind the door and baby." All the things I wanted to say on this occasion were muddled and gone out of mind. I looked at her apprehensively till she was safely down on the platform, helped by her father. Number Five worked wonders within a split second.

I wouldn't have cared if the train had left now. The mother and child stood beside the trunks piled up on the platform. I gazed on my wife, fresh and beautiful, her hair shining, her dress without a wrinkle on it, and her face fresh, with not a sign of fatigue. She wore her usual indigo-coloured silk saree. I looked at her and whispered: "Once again in this saree, still so fond of it," as my father-in-law went back to the compartment to give a final look round. "When will she wake up?" I asked pointing at the child, whom I found enchanting, with her pink face and blue shirt.

"Father is coming down," she said, hinting that I had neglected him and ought to welcome him with a little more ceremony. I obeyed her instantly, went up to my father-in-law and said: "I am very happy, sir, you have come . . ." He smiled and said: "Your wife and daughter got comfortable places, they slept well."

"Did they, how, how? I thought there was such a crowd . . ." My wife answered: "What if there are a lot of others in the compartment? Other people must also travel. I didn't mind it." I knew she was indirectly supporting her father, anticipating my attacks on him for travelling third. "I only thought you might find it difficult to put the child to sleep," I said.

"Oh, everybody made way for us, and we got a whole berth to ourselves," she said, demanding of me by every look and breath that I should be sufficiently grateful to her for it. I turned to him and said: "I'm so happy you managed it so well, sir." He was pleased. He said: "People are ever so good when they see Susila and the baby."

"I hope you will stop with us for at least a week," I said, and looked at my wife for approval. But her father declined the invitation with profuse thanks. He was to be back in his town next day and he was returning by the evening train. He said: "There were three Bombay men, they liked Leela so much that they tried to give her a lot of biscuits. She was only too eager to accept, but I prevented . . ."

"Biscuits are bad for the baby," I said. We moved on. I stretched out my hand: "Let me carry her," I said. My wife declined: "You don't know how to carry a baby yet. You will sprain her." She clasped her closer, and walked off the platform.

A Victoria carriage waited for us outside. Our trunks were stuffed into it, and we squeezed ourselves in. I shared the narrow seat behind the driver with my father-in-law, leaving the other seat for mother and child. Between us were heaped all the trunks and I caught patches of her face through the gaps in the trunks. She talked incessantly about the habits of the infant, enquired about the plan of our house, and asked the names of buildings and streets that we passed.

My mother came down and welcomed her at the gate. She had decorated the threshold with a festoon of green mango leaves and the floor and doorway with white flour designs. She was standing at the doorway and as soon as we got down cried: "Let Susila and the child stay where they are." She had a pan of vermilion solution ready at hand and circled it before the young mother and child, before allowing them to get down from the carriage. After that she held out her arms, and the baby vanished in her embrace.

A look at my mother, her eagerness as she devoured them with her look, and led them into the house, and I was moved by the extraordinary tenderness which appeared in her face. All my dread of yesterday as to how she would prove as a mother-in-law was suddenly eased.

My mother was swamped by this little daughter of mine. She found little time to talk or think of anything else. She fussed over the young mother and the child. She felt it her primary duty to keep the young mother happy and free to look after the little one. The child seemed to be their meeting point; and immediately established a great understanding and harmony between them. All day my mother compelled my wife to stay in her own room and spent her entire time in the kitchen preparing food and drink for her and the child. When the child cried at nights, my mother, sleeping in the hall, sprang up and rocked the cradle, before the young mother should be disturbed. The child still drew nourishment from its mother, and so the latter needed all the attention she could get.

My mother stayed with us the maximum time she could spare—two months—and then returned to the village.

I left the college usually at 4.30 p.m., the moment the last bell rang, and avoiding all interruptions reached home within about twenty minutes. As soon as I turned the street I caught a glimpse of Susila tinkering at her little garden in our compound, or watching our child as she toddled about picking pebbles and mud. . . . It was not in my wife's nature to be demonstrative, but I knew she waited there for me. So I said: "I have taken only twenty minutes and already you are out to look for me!" She flushed when I said this, and covered it up with: "I didn't come out to look for you, but just to play with the child. . . ." My daughter came up and hugged my knees, and held up her hands for my books. I gave her the books. She went up the steps and put them on the table in my room. I followed her in. I took off my coat and shirt, picked up my towel and went to the bathroom, with the child on my arm, as she pointed at the various articles about the house and explained them to me in her own terms. Most of her expressions were still monosyllables, but she made up a great deal by her vigorous gesticulations. She insisted upon watching me as I put my head under the tap. The sight of it thrilled her and she shrieked as water splashed about. I put her safely away from the spray as I bathed, but she stealthily came nearer step by step and tried to catch some of the drops between her fingers. "Ay, child, keep off water." At this she pretended to move off, but the moment I shut my eyes under water and opened them again, she would have come nearer and drenched a corner of her dress, which was a signal for me to turn off the water and dry myself. I rubbed myself, lifted her on my arm, went to my room, and brushed my hair. I did this as a religious duty because I felt myself to be such a contrast to them when I returned in the evening, in my sagging grey cotton suit, with grimy face, and ink-stained fingers, while the mother and daughter looked particularly radiant in the evenings, with their hair dressed and beflowered, faces elegantly powdered.

By the time I reached this stage my wife came out and said: "Your coffee is getting cold. Won't you come in?"

"Yes, yes," and we moved off to our little dining room. An alcove at the end of the dining room served for a shrine. There on a pedestal she kept a few silver images of gods, and covered them with flowers; two small lamps were lit before them every morning. I often saw her standing there with the light in her face, her eyes closed and her lips lightly moving. I was usually amused to see her thus, and often asked what exactly it was that she repeated before her gods. She never answered this question. To this day I have never learnt what magical words she uttered there with closed eyes. Even when I mildly joked about it, "Oh! becoming a yogi!" she never tried to defend herself, but merely treated my references with the utmost indifference. She seemed to have a deep secret life. There hung about this alcove a perpetual smell of burnt camphor and faded flowers.

I sat down on the plank facing the shrine, with the child on my lap. A little plate came up with some delicacy or titbit heaped on it—my tiffin. Susila placed this in front of me and waited to see my reaction. I looked up at her standing before me and asked: "What is this?" She replied: "Find out for yourself, let us see if you recognize it. . . ." As I gazed at it wondering what it might be, the child thrust her hand out for it. I put a little into her mouth while the mother protested: "You are going to spoil her giving her whatever she wants. . . ."

"No, just a little. . . ."

"It will make her sick, she has been eating all sorts of things lately. Don't blame me if she gets sick. . . ."

"Oh, she won't, just a little won't do her any harm. . . ." As Leela held up her hands for more, her mother cried: "No, baby, it won't do. Don't trouble father, come away, come away," and the little one stuck to me fast, avoiding her mother's gaze, and I put my left arm about her and said: "Don't worry about her, I won't give her any more. . . ." As

(37)

I finished what was on the plate Susila asked: "Do you want some more?" This was always a most embarrassing question for me. As I hesitated she asked "Why, is it not good?"

"It is good," I groaned, "but . . ."

"But smells rather smoky, doesn't it? But for the smell it would be perfect," she said. And I couldn't but agree with her. "I prepared such a large quantity thinking you would like it. . . ." She went in and brought out a little more and pushed it on to my plate and I ate with relish just because she was so desperately eager to get me to appreciate her handiwork!

She gave me coffee. We left the kitchen, and sat down in the hall. The child went over to her box in a corner and rummaged its contents and threw them about and became quite absorbed in this activity. My wife sat in the doorway, leaning against the door and watching the street. We spent an hour or more, sitting there and gossiping. She listened eagerly to all the things I told her about my college, work and life. Though she hadn't met a single person who belonged to that world, she knew the names of most of my colleagues and the boys and all about them. She knew all about Brown and what pleased or displeased him. She took sides with me in all my discussions and partisanships, and hated everyone I hated and respected anyone I respected. She told me a great deal about our neighbours, their hopes and fears, and promises and qualities. This talk went on till darkness crept in, and the lights had to be switched on. At the same time the clattering at the toy box ceased. This was a signal that the child would demand attention. She came towards us whimpering and uttering vague complaints. My wife got up and went in to light the oven and cook the dinner, while I took charge of Leela and tried to keep her engaged till her food was ready.

§

On the first of every month, I came home, with ten ten-rupee notes bulging in an envelope, my monthly salary, and placed it in her hand. She was my cash-keeper. And what a ruthless accountant she seemed to be. In her hands, a hundred rupees seemed to do the work of two hundred, and all through the month she was able to give me money when I asked. When I handled my finances independently, after making a few routine savings and payments, I simply paid for whatever caught my eyes and paid off anyone who approached me, with the result that after the first ten days, I went about without money. Now it was in the hands of someone who seemed to understand perfectly where every rupee was going or should go, and managed them with a determined hand. She kept the cash in a little lacquer box, locked it up in her *almirah*, and kept a minute account of it in the last pages of a diary, four years old.

We sat down at my table to draw up the monthly budget and list of provisions. She tore off a sheet of notepaper, and wrote down a complete list—from rice down to mustard. "I have written down the precise quantity, don't change anything as you did once." This was a reference to a slight change that I once attempted to make in her list. She had written down two seers of Bengal gram, but the National Provision Stores could not supply that quantity, and so the shopman suggested he would give half of it, and to make up the purchase, he doubled the quantity of jaggery. All done with my permission. But when I returned home with these, she saw the alterations and was completely upset. I found that there was an autocratic strain in her nature in these matters, and unsuspected depths of rage. "Why has he made this alteration?" she had asked, her face going red. "He didn't have enough of the other stuff," I replied, tired and fatigued by the shopping and on the point of irritability myself. "If he hasn't got a simple thing like Bengal gram, what sort of a shop has he?"

"Come and see it for yourself, if you like," I replied, going into my room. She muttered: "Why should it make you angry? I wonder!" I lay down on my canvas chair, determined to ignore her, and took out a book. She came presently into my room with a paper screw full of sugar and said: "This man has given underweight of sugar. He has cheated you." I lowered the book, frowned at her and asked: "What do you mean?"

"I fear to speak to you if you get angry," she said.

"Who is angry?" I asked. "What is the matter, tell me?"

"I wrote for two measures of sugar, and see this; he has billed for two measures and has actually given a measure and a half. I have measured it just now." She looked at me victoriously, waiting to hear how I was going to answer this charge. I merely said: "He wouldn't do such a thing. You must have some extraordinary measure with you at home."

"Nothing wrong with my measure. Even your mother measured everything with it and said it was correct." So this was a legacy from her mother-in-law. She had taught the girl even this. She had a bronze tumbler, which she always declared was a correct half measure, and she would never recognize other standards and measures. She insisted upon making all her purchases, ghee or oil or milk or salt, with the aid of this measure, and declared that all other measures, including the Government stamped ones, were incorrect, and were kept maliciously incorrect because some municipal members were business men! She used the same tumbler for weighing too, placing it for weight in the scale pan, declaring that the curious thing about the vessel was that by weight too it was exactly half seer, and she would challenge anyone to disprove it. All tradespeople somehow succumbed to this challenge and allowed her to have her own way. She carried this tumbler about wherever she went, and I now found that she had procured a similar one for her daughter-in-law, and had trained her in the use of it.

"Throw away that tumbler and use an honest measure," I said. Susila merely looked at me and said: "Please don't speak so loudly. The child is asleep," and tried to go out of the room. I called her back and said: "If you use an honest measure you will find that others have also done so."

"This National Provisions man is a thief," she cried, "the sooner you change the better." This annoyed me very much. I had known the N.P.S. man for years and liked him. I went all the way to South Extension to patronize his shop, and I liked the man because he was fat and talkative, and Sastri the logic man always said that it was the best shop in the town. I rather prided myself on going to the shop. I liked the fat, thoughtful proprietor. I said: "There is nothing wrong with him. He is the best shop man known. I won't change him. . . ." "I don't know why you should be so fond of him when he is giving undermeasure and rotten stuff . . . " she replied. I was by this time very angry: "Yes, I am fond of him because he is my second cousin," I said with a venomous grin.

Her hatred of him was not mitigated. She said: "You would pay cart hire and go all the way to South Extension to be cheated by him rather than go to a nearer shop. And his rates!" She finished the rest of her sentence with a shiver. "I don't care if he overcharges—I won't drop him," I declared. "Hush, remember the child is sleeping," she said and left the room. I lay in my chair fretting for fifteen minutes and then tried to resume my study, but could read only for five minutes. I got up and went over to the store-room as she was putting away the provisions and articles in their respective tin or glass containers. I stood at the doorway and watched her. I felt a great pity for her; the more because I had not shown very great patience. I asked: "I will return the jaggery if it is too much. Have you absolutely no use for it?" I asked. In answer she pushed before me a glass goblet and said: "This can hold just half a viss of jaggery and not more; which is more than enough for our monthly use. If it is kept in any other place, ants swarm on it," she said. I now saw the logic of her indignation, and by the time our next shopping was done, she had induced me to change over to the Co-operative Stores.

Since then every time the monthly list was drawn up she warned me: "Don't alter anything in it." I followed her list with strict precision, always feeling that one could never be sure what mess any small change might entail. If there were alterations to be made, I rather erred on the side of omission and went again next day after taking her suggestion.

She was very proud of her list. It was precise. Every quantity was conceived with the correct idea as to how long it should last. There were over two dozen different articles to be indented and she listed them with foresight and calculation. She was immensely proud of this ability. She gave me twenty rupees or more for these purchases. I went out to the Co-operative Stores in the Market Road and returned home three hours later followed by a cooly carrying them all in paper bags and bundles, stuffed into a large basket. She always waited for them at the door with unconcealed enthusiasm. The moment I was at the gate she held out her hand for the bill, and hurriedly ran her eyes down the columns checking the figures and prices. "Oh! you have got all the things, and the cost didn't go up above 22-8-0 total . . . slightly better than it was last month. Which item is cheaper this month?" She was in raptures over it. I loved to see her so pleased, and handed her the change to the last pie. She paid the cooly three annas; she would never alter this figure whatever happened. If any one had the hardihood to expect more she declared: "Don't stand there and argue. Be off. Your master has offered you an anna more than you deserve. After all the market is only half a mile away!" She carried the packages to the store-room, and put each in its container, neatly labelled and ranged along a rack. She always needed my assistance to deal with rice. It was the bulkiest bag. It was my set dùty on these days to drag the gunny sack along to the store, lift it and empty it into a zinc drum. I invited her displeasure if I didn't do it carefully. If any rice scattered accidentally on the floor, she said: "I don't know when you will learn economic ways. You are so wasteful. On the quantity you throw about another family could comfortably live."

She watched these containers as a sort of barometer, the

level of their contents indicating the progress of the month. Each had to be at a particular level on a particular date: and on the last date of the month—just enough for another day, when they would be replenished. She watched these with a keen eye like a technician watching an all-important meter at a power house.

All went very well as long as she was reigning supreme in the kitchen—till my mother sent an old lady from the village to cook for us and assist us.

§

One evening we were sitting as usual in the front veranda of the house when an old lady stood at our gate, with a small trunk under her arm, and asked: "Is this teacher Krishnan's house?"

"Yes, who are you, come in. . . ." I opened the gate for her. She looked at me, wrinkling her eyes and said, "Kittu . . . I have seen you as a baby and a boy. How big you have grown!" She came up to the veranda, peered closely into my wife's face and said: "You are our daughter-in-law. I am an old friend of Kamu," she said, referring to my mother by her maiden name. By this time Leela, who had been playing near her box, came out on hearing a new voice. At the sight of her the old lady cried: "So this is Kamu's grandchild!" She picked her up in her arms and fondled her. Susila's heart melted at the sight of it and she said: "Come into the house, won't you?" The old lady went in, sat under the lamp and took out of a corner of her saree a crumpled letter and gave it to me. It was from my mother: "I am sending this letter with an old friend of mine, who was assisting me in household work when you were a baby. She then went away to live with her son. He died last year, and she has absolutely no one to support her. She came to me a few weeks ago in search of work. But I have no need for assistance nowadays. Moreover your father grows rather irritable if he sees any extra person in the house. So I have given her her bus fare and sent

(43)

her on to you. I have always felt that Susila needed an assistant in the house, the baby demanding all the attention she can give. My friend will cook and look after the child. And you can give her whatever salary you like."

While the old lady kept fondling the child, sitting on the floor, I read the letter under the hall light and my wife read it over my shoulder. We looked at each other. There was consternation in her look. There were many questions which she was aching to ask me. I adjourned to my room and she followed me.

"What shall we do?" she asked, looking desperate.

"Why do you look so panicky? We will send her back if you do not want her."

"No, no. How can that be? Your mother has sent her. We have got to have her."

"I think it will be good to have her. All your time is now spent in the kitchen when you are not tending the baby. I don't like you to spend all your time cooking either tiffin or food."

"But I like it. What is wrong in it?" she asked.

"You must spend some more time reading or stitching or singing. Man or woman is not born merely to cook and eat," I said, and added: "You have neglected your books. Have you finished *Ivanhoe?*" She had been trying to get through *Ivanhoe* for years now, and *Lamb's Tales from Shakespeare*. But she never went beyond the fiftieth page. Her library also contained a book of hymns by a Tamil saint, a few select stanzas of Kamba Ramayana, Palgrave's *Golden Treasury* and a leather-bound Bhagavad-Gita in Sanskrit. I knew how fond she was of books. She was always planning how she was going to devour all the books and become the member of some library. But it never became more than an ambition.

In the earlier years of our married life we often sat together with one or other of the books, in the single top-floor room in her father's house, and tried to read. The first half an hour would be wasted because of an irresponsible mood coming over her, which made her laugh at everything: even the most solemn poem would provoke her, especially such poems as were addressed by a lover. "My true love hath my heart and I have his." She would laugh till she became red in the face. "Why can't each keep his own or her own heart instead of this exchange?" She then put out her hand and searched all my pockets saying: "In case you should take away mine!"

"Hush, listen to the poem," I said, and she would listen to me with suppressed mirth and shake her head in disapproval. And then another line that amused her very much was "Oh, mistress mine, where are you roaming?" She would not allow me to progress a line beyond, saying: "I shall die of this poem some day. What is the matter with the woman loafing all over the place except where her husband is?"

However much she might understand or not understand, she derived a curious delight in turning over the pages of a book, and the great thing was that I should sit by her side and explain. While she read the Tamil classics and Sanskrit texts without my help, she liked English to be explained by me. If I showed the slightest hesitation, she would declare: "Perhaps you don't care to explain English unless you are paid a hundred rupees a month for it?"

But all that stopped after the child was born. When the child left her alone, she had to be in the kitchen, and my argument now appealed to her. She said: "But that will mean an extra expense. What shall we pay her?"

"About eight rupees, just what everyone pays, I think," I said.

"Oh, too much," she said. "I'm sure she will waste another eight rupees' worth of things. This is an unnecessary expense," she said. I explained: "Very necessary and we can afford it. In addition to the provident fund, why should we send thirty-five rupees to the savings bank? I think about twenty-five rupees a month for the bank will be more than enough. Many of my friends do not save even five rupees."

"Why do you want to follow their example? We must live within our means, and save enough." She often declared: "When we are old we must never trouble others for help. And remember there is a daughter, for whose marriage we must save."

"When we bring forth some more daughters and sons . . ." I began, and she covered my mouth with her fingers. "You men! what do you care! You would think differently if God somehow made you share the bothers of bringing forth! Where is your promise?" I often reiterated and confirmed our solemn pact that Leela should be our only child. And anything I said otherwise, even in jest, worried her very much.

*   *   *

With the future so much in mind she planned all our finances. She kept a watch over every rupee as it arrived, and never let it depart lightly, and as far as possible tried to end its career in the savings bank.

But now our savings were affected to the extent of at least ten rupees—as she explained "Six rupees, old lady's salary" (Susila stubbornly refused more than that for a year) and "four rupees for all her waste, putting it at a minimum. . . ." She was disconsolate over it for a long time, till I appeased her by saying: "Oh, don't worry about it. When I get some money from examination papers I will give you the whole of it for the savings bank."

In course of time we found that we simply couldn't do without the old lady. She cooked the food for us, tended the child, gave us the necessary courage when the child had fever or stomach-ache and we became distraught; she knew a lot of tricks about children's health, she grew very fond of the child and took her out and kept her very happy. She established herself as a benign elder at home, and for us it meant a great deal. Her devotion to the child enabled me to take my wife twice or thrice a month to a picture, on a walk along the river, or out shopping. My wife grew very fond of her and called her "Granny", so did Leela. But Susila had a price to pay for this pleasure. She lost her supremacy over the kitchen and the store. The levels in the containers at the store went down in other ways than my wife calculated. Susila protested and fought against it for some time, but the old lady had her own way of brushing aside our objections. And Susila adjusted her own outlook in the matter. "Didn't I bargain for a waste of four rupees a month? Well, it is not so hard, because she wastes only three rupees. . . ." Our provision bill fluctuated by only three rupees, and it was a small price to pay for the great company and service of the old lady, who lived on one meal a day, just a handful of cooked rice and buttermilk. It was a wonder how she found the energy for so much activity. My wife often sat down with her in order to induce her to eat well, but it was of no avail.

§

I sat in my room, at the table. It was Thursday and it was a light day for me at college—only two hours of work in the afternoon, and not much preparation for that either. *Pride and Prejudice* for a senior class, non-detailed study, which meant just reading it to the boys. And a composition class. I sat at my table as usual after morning coffee looking over the books ranged on the table and casually turning over the pages of some exercise books. "Nothing to do. Why not write poetry? Ages since I wrote anything?" My conscience had a habit of asserting itself once in six months and reminding me that I ought to write poetry. At such moments I opened the bottommost drawer of my table and pulled out a note book of about five hundred pages, handsomely bound. I had spent nearly a week at a local press getting this done some years ago. Its smooth pages contained my most cherished thoughts on life and nature and humanity. In addition to shorter fragments that I wrote at various times on a miscellany of topics, it contained a long unfinished poem on an epic scale to which I added a few dozen lines whenever my conscience stirred in me. I always fancied that I was born for a poetic career and some day I hoped to take the world by storm with the publication. Some of the pieces were written in English and some in Tamil. (I hadn't yet made up my mind as to which language was to be enriched with my contributions to its literature, but the language was unimportant. The chief thing seemed to be the actual effort.) I turned over the pages looking at my previous writing. The last entry was several months ago, on nature. I felt satisfied with it but felt acute discomfort on realizing that I had hardly done anything more than that. To-day I was going to make up for all lost time; I took out my pen, dipped it in ink, and sat hesitating. Everything was ready except a subject. What should I write about?

My wife had come in and was stealthily watching the pages over my shoulder. As I sat biting the end of my pen, she remarked from behind me: "Oh, the poetry book is out: why are you staring at a blank page?" Her interruption was always welcome. I put away my book, and said: "Sit down," dragging a stool nearer. "No, I'm going away. Write your poetry. I won't disturb you. You may forget what you wanted to write." "I have not even thought of what to write," I said. "Some day I want to fill all the pages of this book and then it will be published and read all over the world." At this she turned over the leaves of the notebook briskly and laughed: "There seem to be over a thousand pages, and you have hardly filled the first ten."

"The trouble is I have not enough subjects to write on," I confessed. She drew herself up and asked: "Let me see if you can write about me."

"A beautiful idea," I cried. "Let me see you." I sat up very attentively and looked at her keenly and fixedly like an artist or a photographer viewing his subject. I said: "Just move a little to your left please. Turn your head right. Look at me straight here. That's right. . . . Now I can write about you. Don't drop your lovely eyelashes so much. You make me forget my task. Ah, now, don't grin please. Very good, stay as you are and see how I write now, steady. . . ." I drew up the notebook, ran the fountain pen hurriedly over it and filled a whole page beginning:

> "She was a phantom of delight
> When first she gleamed upon my sight:
> A lovely apparition, sent
> To be a moment's ornament."

It went on for thirty lines ending:

> "And yet a spirit still, and bright
> With something of an angel-light."

I constantly paused to look at her while writing, and said: "Perfect. Thank you. Now listen."

"Oh, how fast you write!" she said admiringly.

"You will also find how well I've written. Now listen," I said, and read as if to my class, slowly and deliberately, pausing to explain now and then.

"I never knew you could write so well."

"It is a pity that you should have underrated me so long; but now you know better. Keep it up," I said. "And if possible don't look at the pages, say roughly between 150 and 200 in, the *Golden Treasury*. Because someone called Wordsworth has written similar poems." This was an invitation for her to run in and fetch her copy of the *Golden Treasury* and turn over precisely the forbidden pages. She scoured every title and first line and at last pitched upon the original. She read it through, and said: "Aren't you ashamed to copy?"

"No," I replied. "Mine is entirely different. He had written about someone entirely different from my subject."

"I wouldn't do such a thing as copying."

"I should be ashamed to have your memory," I said. "You have had the copy of the *Golden Treasury* for years now, and yet you listened to my reading with gaping wonder! I wouldn't give you even two out of a hundred if you were my student." At this point our conversation was interrupted by my old clock. It burst in upon us all of a sudden. It purred and bleated and made so much noise that it threw us all into confusion. Susila picked it up and tried to stop it without success, till I snatched Taine and smothered it.

"Now, why did it do it?" she demanded. I shook my head. "Just for pleasure," I replied. She gazed on its brown face and said: "It is not even showing the correct time. It is showing two o'clock, four hours ahead! Why do you keep it on your table?" I had no answer to give. I merely said: "It has been with me for years, poor darling!"

"I will give it away this afternoon—a man comes to buy all old things."

"No, no, take care, don't do it . . ." I warned. She didn't answer, but merely looked at it and mumbled: "This is not the first time. When you are away it starts bleating after I have rocked the cradle for hours and made the child sleep, and I don't know how to stop it. It won't do for our house. It is a bother. . . ."

That evening when I returned home from college the first thing I noticed was that my room looked different. My table had lost its usual quality and looked tidy, with all books dusted and neatly arranged. It looked like a savage, suddenly appearing neatly trimmed and groomed. The usual corner with old newspapers and magazines piled up was clean swept. The pile was gone. So was the clock on the table. The table looked barren without it. For years it had been there. With composition books still under my arm, I searched her out. I found her in the bathroom, washing the child's hands. "What have you done with my clock?" I asked. She looked up and asked in answer: "How do you like your room? I have cleaned and tidied it up. What a lot of rubbish you gathered there! Hereafter on every Thursday . . ."

"Answer first, where is the clock?" I said.

"Please wait, I will finish the child's business first and then answer."

I stood at the bathroom doorway and grimly waited. She finished the child's business and came out bearing her on her arm. While passing me she seized the child's hand and tapped me under the chin with it and passed on without a word to her room. She later met me in my room as I sat gloomily gazing at the table.

"Why have you not had your tiffin or wash?" she asked, coming up behind and gently touching my shoulder.

"I don't want any tiffin," I snapped.

"Why are you so angry?" she asked.

"Who asked you to give away that clock?" I asked.

"I didn't give it away. That man gave me twelve annas for it—a very high price indeed."

"Now you are a . . . ." I began. I looked at the paper corner and wailed: "You have given away those papers too! There were old answer papers there. . . ."

"Yes, I saw them," she said. "They were four years old. Why do you want old papers?" she asked. I was too angry to answer. "You have no business to tamper with my things," I said. "I don't want any tiffin or coffee." I picked up my coat, put it on and rushed out of the house, without answering her question: "Where are you going?"

I went straight back to the college. I had no definite plan. There was no one in the college. I peeped into the debating hall, hoping there might be somebody there. But the evening was free from all engagements. I remembered that I hadn't had my coffee. I walked about the empty corridors of the college. I saw the servant and asked him to open our common room. I sent him to fetch me coffee and tiffin from the restaurant. I opened my locker and took out a few composition books. I sat correcting them till late at night. I heard the college clock strike nine. I then got up and retraced my way home. I went about my work with a business-like air. I took off my coat, went at great speed to the bathroom and washed. I first took a peep into my wife's room. I saw her rocking the baby in the cradle. I went into the kitchen and told the old lady: "Have the rest dined?"

The old lady answered: "Susila waited till eight-thirty."

I was not interested in this. Her name enraged me. I snapped: "All right, all right, put up my leaf and serve me. I only wanted to know if the child had eaten." This was to clear any misconception anyone might entertain that I was interested in Susila.

I ate in silence. I heard steps approaching, and told myself: "Oh, she is coming." I trembled with anxiety, lest she should be going away elsewhere. I caught a glimpse of her as she came into the dining room. I bowed my head, and went on with my dinner unconcerned, though fully aware that she was standing before me, dutifully as ever, to see that I was served correctly. She moved off to the kitchen, spoke some words to the old lady, and came out, and softly moved back to her own room. I felt angry: "Doesn't even care to wait and see me served. She doesn't care. If she cared, would she sell my clock? I must teach her a lesson."

After dinner I was back in my room and sat down at my table. I had never been so studious at any time in my life. I took out some composition books. I noticed on a corner of my table a small paper packet. I found enclosed in it a few coins. On the paper was written in her handwriting:

| Time-piece | 12 annas |
| Old paper | 1 rupee |

| Total | One rupee and twelve annas. |

I felt furious at the sight of it. I took the coins and went over to her room. The light was out there. I stood in the doorway and muttered: "Who cares for this money? I can do without it." I flung it on her bed and returned to my room.

Later, as I sat in my room working, I heard the silent night punctuated by sobs. I went to her room and saw her lying with her face to the wall, sobbing. I was completely shaken. I didn't bargain for this. I watched her silently for a moment, and collected myself sufficiently to say: "What is the use of crying, after committing a serious blunder?" Through her sobs, she sputtered: "What do you care, what use it is or not. If I had known you cared more for a dilapidated clock." She didn't finish her sentence, but broke down and wept bitterly. I was baffled. I was in an anguish myself. I wanted to take her in my arms and comfort her. But there was a most forbidding pride within me. I merely said: "If you are going to talk and behave like a normal human being, I can talk to you. I can't stand all this nonsense."

"You go away to your room. Why do you come and abuse me at midnight?" she said.

"Stop crying, otherwise people will think a couple of lunatics are living in this house. . . ."

I went back to my room—a very determined man. I lay on a mat, trying to sleep, and spent a miserable and sleepless night.

We treated each other like strangers for the next forty-eight hours—all aloof and bitter. The child looked on this with puzzlement, but made it up by attending to her toys and going to the old lady for company. It was becoming a torture. I could stand no more of it. I had hoped Susila would try to make it up, and that I could immediately accept it. But she confined herself to her room and minded her business with great concentration and never took notice of me. I caught a glimpse of her face occasionally and found that her eyes were swollen. I felt a great pity for her, when I saw her slender neck, as she was going away from the bathroom. I blamed myself for being such a savage. But I couldn't approach her. The child would not help us either; she was too absorbed in her own activities. It came to a point when I simply could not stand any more of it. So the moment I returned home from college next evening I said to her, going to her room:

"Let us go to a picture. . . ."

"What picture?" she asked.

"*Tarzan*—at Variety Hall. You will like it very much. . . ."

"Baby?"

"The old lady will look after her. We shall be back at nine. Dress up. . . ." I was about to say "Look sharp," but

I checked myself and said: "There is a lot of time. You needn't hustle yourself."

"No, I'll be ready in ten minutes . . ." she said rising.

By the time we were coming out of the Variety Hall that night we were in such agreement and showed such tender concern for each other's views and feelings that we both wondered how we could have treated each other so cruelly. "I thought we might buy a new clock, that's why I gave away the old one," she said.

"You did the best thing possible," I said. "Even in the hostel that wretched clock worried everyone near about. I am glad you have rid me of it."

"They make such beautiful ones nowadays," she said.

"Yes, yes, right. We will go out and buy one tomorrow evening," I said. When we reached home we decided that we should avoid quarrelling with each other since, as she put it, "They say such quarrels affect a child's health."

CHAPTER THREE

On the occasion of our child's third birthday, my father wrote to say that he would advance me money to buy a house in Malgudi or to build one. He did not think it was very wise to go on living in a rented house. This offer made us very happy. I and my wife sat down and carried on endless discussions to decide which would be better, whether a built house or a site on which to build. "A room all for myself where I can sit and spin out great poetry," I said.

"Well, some place where you can be free from my presence?" she asked. "Why don't you be plain?" "No, no," I replied awkwardly.

"I'm not eager to thrust my company on you either," she said. "I am as eager to have a separate room."

"In that case, I don't want one," I replied. "Why should both of us have separate rooms?"

"Are you fighting?" the little one asked, gazing at us bewildered. "You are always scolding mother," she said looking at me, and I felt unhappy at this thrust.

We agreed to go out on the following Sunday morning to Lawley Extension to choose a house or a site.

We were up with the dawn. The old cook had gone out to see a relation on the previous evening. I had to light the fire and boil the water for coffee while Susila bathed, dressed, and prepared herself for the outing. As I sat struggling with smoke in my eyes and nostrils, she appeared at the kitchen doorway, like a vision, clad in her indigo saree, and hair gleaming and jasmine covered. I looked at her indigo saree and smiled to myself. She noticed it and asked "Why that?"

"Nothing, nothing," I said with a cold damp in my nose. My voice was thick. "What is wrong with this saree? It is as good as another!" she said.

"Yes, yes," I replied. "That is why I say you should use it more sparingly, otherwise you will wear it out. . . ." Her eyes sparkled with joy; she spread the fragrance of jasmine more than ever. "The divine creature!" I reflected within myself, looking at her tall, slim figure.

> "She was a phantom of delight
> When first she gleamed upon my sight."

My mind unconsciously quoted—the habit of an English teacher. The water reached boiling point and was lifting and throwing down the lid. All around the kitchen lay scattered faggots and burnt matchsticks and coal. Smoke still hung in the air. I smelt of coffee powder. "Five spoons of powder and two tumblers of water, am I right?" I asked. She suddenly pushed me aside and said: "Now, get ready. Let us be off. I will attend to this. . . ."

I went away, and returned in half an hour ready and dressed. She gave me coffee. The maidservant had come. Susila placed a tumbler of milk on a teapoy outside and told the servant: "Give this to the baby when she wakes up. Make her drink off the whole of it. Keep her engaged till the old lady returns. She will be back at about eight. Tell her that I will bring her fine toys and biscuits. . . ."

She threw a look at the sleeping baby, drew a blanket over her, and said "Sit by her side, so that when she wakes up she may not cry."

As we stepped out of the house, she said: "I hope the child won't cry. . . ."

"Don't keep bothering about her. She will be all right. You will be spoiling her if you bother so much. She must learn to exist by herself. . . ." My wife merely smiled at me. "I'm confident that the old woman will keep her happy, but she must come back in time."

A fresh morning breeze blew. I took in a deep breath and said: "Do you know how I used to love the early morning walk along the river when I was in the hostel. . . . There is a magic in the atmosphere. . . ." I was highly elated. The fresh sun, morning light, the breeze, and my wife's presence, who looked so lovely—even an unearthly loveliness—her tall form, dusky complexion, and the small diamond ear-rings—Jasmine, Jasmine. . . . "I will call you Jasmine, hereafter," I said. "I've long waited to tell you that. . . ."

"Remember, we are in a public road and don't start any of your pranks here," she warned, throwing at me a laughing glance. Her eyes always laughed—there was a perpetual smile in her eyes. "The soul laughs through the eyes, it is the body which laughs with lips . . ." I remarked. "What are you saying?" she asked. "Nothing," I replied.

"I hope you've not forgotten that we are in a public road?" "What I say is perfectly innocent, no harm even if repeated on a public platform." We were now in Market Road. Vehicles were moving about. The market was stirring into activity.

People as they passed threw a glance at us, some students saluted me. I said, "My boys, good fellows. . . ." "Must be, because they salute you," she said.

We were now passing before Bombay Ananda Bhavan, a restaurant. "Shall we go in?" she asked. I was only too delighted. I led her in. A number of persons were sitting in the dark hall over their morning coffee. There was a lot of din and clanging of vessels. Everybody turned and stared, the presence of a woman, particularly at that hour, being so very unusual. I felt rather shy. She went ahead, and stood in the middle of the hall not knowing where to go. A waiter appeared. "Here Mani," I hailed, knowing this boy, a youngster from Malabar, who had served me tiffin for several years now. I felt very proud of his acquaintance.

Mani said, "Family room upstairs, follow me." We followed him. There was a single room upstairs, with a wooden, marble-topped table and four chairs. The walls were lined as usual with fancy, coloured tiles.

"These marbles are so nice," my wife said, with simple joy, running her fingers over them. "How smooth!"

"Do you know they are used only in bathrooms in civilized cities; they are called bathroom tiles."

"They are so nice, why should these be used only for bathrooms?"

"Do you think those bathrooms are like ours?"

"Bathrooms are bathrooms wherever they may be . . ." she replied.

"No, no, a bathroom is very much unlike the smoke-ridden, wet, dripping bathing-place we have."

"I try to keep it as neat as possible, and yet you think it is not good," she remarked.

"I didn't mean that."

"I think you did mean it." I didn't like to spoil a good morning with a debate. So I agreed: "I am sorry. Forgive and forget."

"All right," she said. She stretched her arms back and touched the wall behind her and said, "I like these tiles, so fine and smooth! When we have a house of our own, won't you have some of them fixed like that on our walls?"

"With pleasure, but not in the hall, they are usually put up only in the bathrooms," I pleaded.

"What if they are! People who like them for bathrooms may have them there, others if they want them elsewhere. . . ."

At this moment Mani appeared carrying a tray of eatables. "How quickly he has brought these!" she remarked: this was her first visit to Bombay Ananda Bhavan. Its magnitude took her breath away. Her eyes sparkled like a child's.

She tried to eat with a spoon. She held it loosely and tipped the thing into her mouth from a distance. I suggested,

"Put it away if you can't manage with it." She made a wry face at the smell of onion: "I can't stand it—" she said. "I know. I know," I replied. "What a pity." It was careless of me. I knew that she hated onions but had taken no care to see that they were not given to her. I reproached myself: I called for the boy vociferously and commanded: "Have that removed, bring something without onion." I behaved as if I were an elaborate, ceremonial host. I wanted to please her. Her helplessness, innocence, and her simplicity moved me very deeply. "I will give you something nice to eat." I gave elaborate instructions to the boy. She mentioned her preference, a sweet, coloured drink—like a child's taste once again, I thought. I fussed about her till she said, "Oh, leave me alone," with that peculiar light dancing in her eyes. She said, "Shall we take something for the child?" I didn't like to spoil a good morning with contradictions, but I did not approve of giving hotel stuff to the baby. So I said with considerable diplomacy: "We will buy her some nice biscuits. She likes them very much."

Nearly an hour later we came out of the hotel. I proposed that we should engage a *jutka* for going to Lawley Extension, but she preferred to walk. She said that she'd be happy to walk along the river. "My dear girl," I said, "Lawley Extension is south and this river north of the town. We are going to the Extension on business."

"Please, please," she pleaded recklessly. "I must wash my feet in the river to-day." I was in the mood to yield completely to her wishes. So I agreed though it meant walking a couple of miles in the opposite direction.

It was a most exhilarating walk down the river. She splashed her feet in the water, rested under the banyan, heaped up sand and kept muttering, "How the little girl would love it if only she could be brought here! I think she will simply roll in the sand. But we must take care not to let her go near the water."

I watched her once again. . . . "Do you know how I used to spend all my morning here when I was in the hostel. . . . I used to get up at dawn. . . ."

"You could continue it even now. . . . I hope you will not say I'm responsible for your giving up the good habit," she said. I laughed. "It doesn't look very important now, that is all; I did it for some time then; no compulsion to repeat the same thing for ever, even if it is good."

When we were ready to go back I suggested, "We must go on an all-India tour sometime. I will take you with me."

"Promise?" she asked.

"Absolutely," I said. "I will take you also to England and Europe if I make a lot of money out of the books I am going to write."

"What about the child?"

"She will be grown up by then," I replied. "We can leave her with her grandparents. You must see everything." I imagined, even as I spoke, how she would touch the marble of Taj, stand astounded before the snow-covered Himalayas, and before the crowd and magnitude of European cities.

§

We left the river and went to Lawley Extension in a *jutka*. When we got down there, she looked a little tired. Her face had a slight flush. "We have to walk a little here," I warned her. "Do you think I can't?" she asked, and went forward.

Lawley Extension formed the southernmost portion of the town, and consisted of well laid-out residential buildings, lining the neat roads and crossroads. It was the very end of the town, beyond which passed the Trichy trunk road, shaded with trees. At one time, only those with very high incomes could have residences there, but about five years ago, under a new scheme, the extension developed farther south; even beyond the trunk road the town was extending. There was a general scramble for these sites and houses, which received an uninterrupted southern breeze blowing across the fields, a most satisfactory outlook aesthetically, the corn fields, which were receding in the face of the buildings, waving in sunlight. "I shall have to cycle up to the college, but it doesn't matter. We shall have a most enchanting view before us, we won't know that we are in a town." I became very enthusiastic. A friend of mine, Sastri of the logic section, had promised me his help in choosing a house. He was the moving spirit of this new extension, secretary of the Building and Acquisition Society, and a most energetic "extender". No one could have believed that he had so much business capacity —his main occupation being logic. He was a marvellous man—a strange combination of things, at one end "undistributed middle", "definition of knowledge", "syllogisms", and at the other he had the spirit of a pioneer. His was the first building in the New Extension, and then he got together a few persons and formed his company, which was chiefly responsible for the growth of this New Extension.

We reached Sastri's house, a small bungalow in a vast compound overgrown with trees. Sastri—a thin grey-haired man—was sitting under a tree digging its roots.

"Hullo, Sastri!" I cried. "I am sorry I'm so late. This lady is responsible for it," I said pointing to my wife. Sastri came up, picking the mud off his hands.

"So glad you have brought your wife, I hear lots of complaints that you don't bring her out," said Sastri.

"Oh, there is a small child to be looked after," I replied.

"You could bring her out too."

"Oh, it is not so easy." I began to visualize all the difficulties in an instant: the protection, ceaseless attention and all the rest of it. "Father take me up, I can't walk." "Father, put me down, I don't like to be carried." "I'm hungry," and "I won't eat anything."

"It is not so easy," I said.

"Why, why?" asked the logician.

"You see," I began, but realized how utterly hopeless it

would be to explain it all to him—this childless man would not understand the complications. I changed the subject: "I hope you will take us to see some houses."

"Come up, come up, we will discuss it." He took me in and seated me in the veranda, on a discoloured rattan chair, which pricked my back. Sastri said: "Still interested in houses? Why don't you buy a site and build a good house? I have a beautiful site for you up there."

"Oh, I can't wait for all the bricks and mortar to take shape. I don't know anything of house building, too much bother."

"Leave it all to me," Sastri said. "I will do it." He had taken upon himself this task for scores of people, and some uncharitable ones remarked that he made a better living out of it than as a logic lecturer.

"I've no patience to wait, my dear fellow," I pleaded. "I can't stand all the nuisance. I want a house at the moment I think of it."

"Very well, I'll show you some. See how you like them. If you don't like any of them, you may just accept my other suggestion." He sent his servant to fetch the building contractor: a dark man, with a moustache, and a red vermilion mark on his forehead. "Sit down, Swamy, can those houses be seen to-day?" Sastri asked.

"Yes, yes, I will send the boy to keep them open." He despatched a boy.

Sastri's wife had given us lemon squash to drink, and refreshed, Susila started out once again with us.

Sastri said: "We will have to do a little walking. I hope the lady won't feel too fatigued."

"No, no, not at all. I can walk miles," Susila replied.

I was walking on between Sastri and the contractor, who were full of house-building talk. A little later I turned and noticed that Susila had fallen back, unable to keep pace with us. I stopped and joined her. Standing beside her, I felt like calling her "Jasmine" once again. I whispered: "We are going to see some very nice houses, are you pleased?"

"Yes, yes."

"You must tell me which of them you like best. . . ."

"Yes," she replied. I whispered: "Don't worry about the child, she will be quite happy."

"If she starts crying for some reason or other, no one can stop her. The old lady will not be able to manage," she said.

"Oh, don't imagine all those things," I pleaded. I lowered my voice still further and said, "Jasmine . . ." She suppressed a smile that came on her lips, her eyes flashed a mild reproof.

We came before a row of very small houses—each with a very narrow suffocating veranda, and a front garden, half a dozen monotonously alike.

"Do you like this pattern?" Sastri asked me. I looked at my wife. She said: "The child will lose her way not knowing which is her house—they are all alike. Why are these so alike?" She shook her head. Sastri added: "The second house is for sale." I said: "Can't we see some other pattern? This is too small." A young boy held the door open. Sastri said: "Come in and see the house. No harm in seeing the house." He was a connoisseur in houses and expected others to be the same. The contractor added: "Yes, yes, you must see different types before deciding." "What an amount of banality surrounds the purchase of a house! How much we have to bear before we are through with it," I reflected. The contractor commanded the boy: "Are all the houses open?"

"Yes, master."

"Don't say 'yes'! Keep them open," he said.

"Yes, master," he said.

"You are a careless fool," he added. "I will pluck off your ear if you aren't careful!" "Why does this man bully the young fellow unnecessarily?" I reflected. "Some people are made that way. Perhaps, if a census on this subject were taken, ten thousand persons would be found to be bullying

ten thousand others every minute all over the world. . . ."
I wanted the boy to be saved further persecution and so asked
the contractor: "What is the width of this veranda?"

"Forty-four inches. . . ."

Sastri asked: "What do you think of it?"

"I don't like it. It is no use having such a small house," I
replied.

"But the price!" Sastri said with a knowing smile. "The
best at twelve hundred!"

"Oh, Sastri, how did this house-salesmanship get into your
blood, instead of logic?" I reflected.

At last we came to a house which seemed attractive. It had
a wide compound, broad windows, and a general appearance
of spaciousness and taste. All the doors and the walls looked
fresh with paint. As we turned the street, Susila saw the contractor's boy standing at the gate, and asked with a great
thrill: "Is that also ours?" It was very attractive with two
jasmine creepers trained over an arch on the gateway. It was
full of flowers. The gates moved on silent hinges. As we were
about to go under the arch I lightly touched her arm and
pointed at the jasmine creeper. I told the contractor: "I
would love to call this the Jasmine Home, its perfume greets
us even as we enter." The contractor was pleased. "I hope
you will like it inside too," he said.

A few steps led up to the veranda—a fairly deep and cool
veranda, with a short parapet. Susila sat on the parapet. I
sat beside her and said: "Someone with taste has planned it."
Sastri looked greatly pleased that a house of his selection
had received such approval. The main door was opened, and
we inspected the house room by room. A hall, four rooms, in
addition to the kitchen, a pleasing light blue paint on all the
walls inside the house. Susila and I were thrilled. We went
away by ourselves, lingered in every room, and visualized ourselves as its future occupants.

"What's the price?" she asked.

"Must be within our figure, otherwise they would not have brought us here."

"Plenty of space for the child to play. She can simply run about just as she likes. Those parapets on the veranda are a good idea to prevent her from falling off."

"There is plenty of space for guests too. The grandparents may also come and stay with us quite comfortably. The small room in the front veranda will be my study. I shall write immense quantities of poetry when I settle here, I think."

"Sometime my mother must come and stay with us," she said. "She has always blamed us for living in a rented house. She will be very happy, I am sure."

"You must also have the room next to mine as all your own—if you like I will have coloured marble tiles fitted along the walls."

"So that you may call it the bathroom, I suppose," she remarked.

We joined the other two sitting on the veranda, and discussed the price and other details: "It was occupied only for three months after it was built and changed hands."

"Why?" I asked, trying to appear as a man of great business wisdom. Sastri replied, looking serious, "I've not enquired. Have you any idea?" The contractor said: "I built the house for the gentleman, and the family went away and settled in Madras. Rich people don't usually mind these things."

"Of course, without doubt," replied the contractor. "This is at the end of the town, that is the chief reason. . . ." It was a fact. It was really the very last house, in the last cross-road of the New Extension. Fields of corn stretched away in front of the house, and far beyond it, a cluster of huts of the next village, and beyond it all stood up the blue outlines of Mempi Mountains. It was a lovely prospect. I stood looking at it and said: "A magnificent view, only a buffalo could be insensible to it."

"Is this a mosquito-ridden place?" I asked.

"Some parts of the year. . . . The best thing to do is to sleep under a net."

"I feel suffocated under a mosquito net. I prefer a mosquito bite," Sastri said.

The contractor said: "I am sixty-five years old and I have never been under a mosquito net! I've never had malaria even once."

"Really?" Sastri asked, greatly impressed.

"A fact. You ask my old mother if you like," replied the contractor. "I think all this stuff about mosquitoes is nonsense. As if there were no mosquitoes in the days of our grandfathers." Susila found the talk boring: "I'll go and have a look round the compound," she said. I got up. Susila replied: "No, you needn't come. I'll just see the compound and backyard, and return." She started out. I followed her a few paces. "Why do you want to go?" I asked. "Shall I follow you?"

"Oh, won't you let me alone even for a few minutes?" she whispered. "Nobody will carry me off. I can look after myself!" She went away. I returned to my friends, and continued our talk. I promised to write to my father, and complete the transaction at an early date. They fixed the coming Wednesday as a date for further discussions. I took Sastri aside and requested him to settle the price favourably. "Leave it to me. I will cut down at least five hundred," Sastri assured me. My mind was in a whirl—I was already tremendously excited. "We must move in within a month, if possible," I reflected.

Half an hour passed. "What is Susila doing with herself so long?" I thought. I jumped down, saying: "Wait a minute, please," and ran round to the backyard.

I noticed as I went along what a lot of space there was for making a small manageable garden. The fertility of the surrounding fields had affected this place too and there was a growth of pleasant green grass and one or two uncared-for bushes of leucas—which put forth small, whitish flowers. "This poor plant is the first to be removed whenever a garden is made, because it grows naturally—but I shall make a point of preserving it." I stopped and plucked a flower. I wondered what ideas Susila had for the garden, and decided that the bulk of it should be left to her care and management. "I am sure she is thinking of a very grand kitchen garden in the backyard . . ." I told myself. I went on to the backyard, where a few young cocoanut trees threw a sparse shade around. Susila was not to be seen. I looked for her and called, "Susila! Susila!" She answered from somewhere. I called again, and she cried: "Push the door open! I can't open it from this side." I found that her voice came from the other side of a green-painted lavatory door. I gave it a kick and it flew open. Out she came—red and trembling. I looked at her and felt disturbed.

"What—what were you doing here?" I asked. She was panting with excitement. She was still shivering. I seated her on a stone slab nearby. "What is the matter? What is the matter?"

"I went in there. The door was so bright and I thought it'd be clean inside . . . but oh!" she screwed up her face and shuddered, unable to bear the disgust that came with recollection. I felt agitated. "Why did you go there?" I cried. She didn't answer. It was a sad anti-climax to a very pleasing morning. I looked at her feet. "You went in barefoot?" She nodded.

"Where are your sandals?"

"I forgot them at home." I shook my head in despair. "I have told you a hundred times not to come out barefoot. And yet . . ." She merely looked at me without replying. Her face was beaded with perspiration. Her cheeks were flushed. She was still trembling. I melted at the sight of it: "Oh, darling, why did you go there?"

"The door was so bright . . ." she replied softly. "I thought it'd be clean inside too . . . but I couldn't come out after I went in—the door shut by itself with a bang. I thought something terrible had happened. . . . Ah, the flies and other things there!" She was convulsed with disgust. "Oh, oh . . . A fly came and sat on my lip. . . ." She wouldn't bring her lips together. She kept rubbing them with her fingers in an effort to eradicate the touch of the fly. . . . I said: "There is the water tap. Rinse your mouth, and wash your feet, you will be all right. Don't think of it any more." She jumped up on the stone slab, turned the tap on and washed her hands and feet and mouth, again and again. She rubbed her feet on the stone till they were red and till they smarted. It looked as though she would not stop this operation. I said: "You'll hurt yourself, or you may catch a cold. Come away. Don't bother about it any more. You are all right."

We came back to the veranda. Sastri and the contractor were waiting for us. I seated Susila in a clean corner of the veranda and advised her to lean on the wall, and rest. The others observed her flushed face and asked what the matter was. "She visited that lavatory and found it rather unclean," I said. "Oh," the contractor said: "I wish the lady had told us, I'd have asked her not to go there. This is one of the curses of the place. It is so far out and so near the field and village that all kinds of people passing this way stop here for shelter, and they foul a lavatory beyond description. . . . This is not the first time such a complaint has come to us."

"When the house is occupied?" I asked.

"Oh no, no trouble then, only when it is vacant. It's so difficult to engage a caretaker for every little place, though there is a peon going round to see these things at least once a day."

After resting for about half an hour Susila got up and said: "I feel all right."

Sastri and the contractor went ahead. I kept my wife company, watching her every movement anxiously. When we approached Sastri's house, he suggested: "Won't you come in

(68)

for a moment? The lady can have a little coffee. She looks tired." Susila declined this with a smile.

"Oh no, thanks, we will be going, it is late," I said. "We will meet on Wednesday."

We walked down the crossroad. When the presence of the other two was withdrawn, I grew elaborately fussy—I asked her for the hundredth time if she was feeling all right. As we were passing into the main road, we saw a small, newly-built temple. "They have built a beautiful temple for this place, so near our house. So thoughtful of them . . ." I said. "We will go in," she said, "and see the god."

"Most certainly."

There was an old woman sitting on a gunny sack at the temple gate, selling offerings. "Buy something for the god," she entreated.

"What temple is this?" Susila asked.

"*Srinivasa*—the greatest god; you need not visit Thiru-pathi Hills to see him, if you visit him here—he grants all your boons and blesses all your efforts. . . ." She held up a cocoanut, a packet of camphor, plantain, and betel leaves.

"You are both so young and bright. He will bless you with numerous children and may they all be sons . . ." said the old lady.

"Hush," Susila replied: "We have one and we are satisfied with one . . ." she laughed and entered the temple. I was tremendously relieved to see her laugh. We entered the temple hall—a stone pillared hall, smelling of camphor and flowers, cool and shady. There were two bronze lamps burning in the inner sanctuary, illuminating a tall stone image of *Srinivasa*. A priest, wrapped in a shawl, sitting at the foot of the image, rose on seeing us and held up a plate. We placed the offerings on it.

"What a lovely image!" Susila remarked. She brought together her palms and closed her eyes in prayer. I stood watching her. The priest broke the cocoanut, and placed it and the other things at the feet of the image. He lit the camphor, sounded a bell, and circled the flame around the image. In this flickering light the image acquired strange shadows and seemed to stir, and make a movement to bless—I watched my wife. She opened her eyes for a moment. They caught the light of the camphor flame, and shone with an unearthly brilliance. Her cheeks glowed, the rest of her person was lost in the shadows of the temple hall. Her lips were moving in prayer. I felt transported at the sight of it. I shut my eyes and prayed: "God bless this child and protect her." She received the holy water from the priest and touched her lips and eyes, put a vermilion dot on her forehead, and tucked the flower offered to the god in her hair. We stepped out. As we descended the temple steps she muttered: "Only now do I feel quite well again. We must make it a point to visit this temple as often as we can."

"You can visit it every evening when we have taken the new house," I said.

"Yes, yes." I was greatly relieved to see her happy and fit once again. We hailed a passing *jutka*, climbed into it, and sat snugly close. The *jutka* wheels rattled over the cobbles and it lulled us into a mild drowse. We ceased to pass any remarks or comment and settled in a tranquil silence. I studied her face without her knowledge. A great peace had descended on her. "It is God's infinite grace that has given me this girl." The *jutka* was filled with the scent of the jasmine in her hair and the glare of the indigo-coloured saree.

As we passed the Market Road, she reminded me, "You have promised to buy biscuits and a doll for the child." We stopped the carriage before Novelty House. I dashed in and came out bearing a biscuit packet, a doll and a toy engine.

When we reached home we found the child playing very happily with the cook and a child from the next house. We heard her voice, over and above the rattle of the carriage wheels, when we were still two houses away. As soon as the carriage stopped, Leela came out running. Her mother took her up in her arms immediately, and gave her the doll, train and the biscuits. Leela's friend from the next house was also there. Leela said to her: "You can go home now, my mother is come." The friend said: "All right, . . ." and hesitated, casting a look on the game they had been playing. . . . They had raised a building with wooden blocks, and various small utensils filled with water and grains and flowers and leaves were strewn about the small hall—they had been playing "Home Keeping" and calling on each other.

"Yes, she was a very fine child to-day. When mother is at home, she gives such a lot of trouble over food! She was my sweet child to-day," said the old cook.

"Did she ask where we were?"

"Ah, didn't she? Every few minutes asking and asking why her mother had gone out without telling her. She is a smart child."

"Why did you go away mother, at night?" the little one asked. "When I opened my eyes, I didn't see you but her." The cook shook with laughter: "What a lot of speech she has learnt! She is going to defeat all the others in your family in speech, madam."

"Why did you go away, mother?" the little girl asked. Her mother threw herself on the floor, even without changing her dress. "Too tired for anything now. I won't get up, whatever happens, without resting for another half an hour. . . ."

"You must eat your food first," the old cook began.

"No, get up, get up, Susila," I said. But she begged to be allowed to rest for half an hour.

"Where did you go, mother, without telling me?"

"To buy a house for you."

"What is it made of?"

"Stone and lime."

"Is it so high?" she indicated with her hand a yard in height and said: "I want one which is small and can be put in the trunk."

"I mean a real big house like this," said the mother.

"This is our house?" the child asked.

(71)

"Another one, more beautiful—Oh! You can play all day with plants."

"Can I play in mud?"

"Oh, yes, it's very clean and nice. . . ."

"My friend must also come with me." She carried on this conversation sitting on her mother, clutching the doll and the train, and eating a biscuit.

I busied myself for half an hour in my room, and came out. I still found my wife lying on the floor: "Oh, why have you flung yourself down in this manner? Go and change. We will eat. . . ."

"Leave me alone for a little, please," she pleaded.

I felt her temples with my fingers: "If this small excursion exhausts you so much, I don't know what I can do with you when we go on our North Indian travel."

"I will be all right then."

"You will be better if you eat a hearty meal at once."

She begged, "Please, don't compel me. The thought of food upsets me. Go and finish your food first, and don't wait for me." I protested at the idea and went away to my room. "I can also take it later with you. I'm not particularly hungry. I think the hotel stuff has not agreed with you."

The child snuggled close to her mother and clung to her neck. I said: "Don't trouble your mother."

"I'm not troubling her. I'm making her headache go," replied the child.

I went away to my study and stood for a moment gazing at my table. My wife had given up all attempts at tidying up my room, and it had lapsed into the natural state of my hostel days. Once again all Milton and Shakespeare and Bradley jostled each other in a struggle for existence. There were four library books on my table which had been overdue, accumulating fines and bringing me fierce reminders from the librarian, but which I had not opened even once. There were the latest books on Plato, Swinburne, modern poetry, and others which the librarian had forced on me in one of his hospitable moods. I realized that I used to read better when I was in the hostel and had not become the head of a family. Nor were my hours spent in chatting with my wife or watching the child play or in running about on shopping errands. My conscience troubled me whenever I thought of it. "I will not waste half an hour, but will get through this stuff on Plato." I picked up the book and lounged in my canvas chair. "Plato's idealism . . ." I read. "Sickening fellows. Why won't they leave Plato alone? For the thousandth time someone restating Plato—I don't like this book. I shall return it." I put it away. The other book too I found unreadable.

I found that I had spent half an hour in these attempted studies. I put away the books. I leaned back in my chair, hoping I should be called. There was no sound in the house. I got up and went to the hall. I saw the mother and the child fast asleep where they lay. My first impulse was to waken Susila. I watched her for a moment. "Too tired, let her sleep for a while," I reflected. "I will dine first, she may wake up and join me." I went to the dining room; and sat down before the leaf. The old cook served me. "Where is . . ." she began in her croaking voice. "Hush, not so loudly. She's asleep" I said. "She will wake up presently." I went through my meal, and tiptoed out to the bathroom, washed my hands, and while I dried them, stood near her and watched. Her lips were slightly parted. "Is she still reluctant to bring her lips together?" I asked myself. I sat by her side, and gently touched her eyelids with the tip of my finger. She opened her eyes, at once saw the child asleep by her side, clutching her toys, and disengaged herself gently and sat up. I said: "I've had my food; I felt hungry. Won't you come and eat?"

I led her to the bathroom, and gently splashed a little cold water on her face. I took her to the kitchen, seated her before her leaf, and sat by her side. She obeyed implicitly without saying a word. The old lady muttered, "You should never delay your food so long. An empty stomach makes poison." She served some vegetables and dhal. Susila murmured, "None of these. Only a little rice and buttermilk for me." After due protests she was allowed to have her choice. She sat gazing at her leaf. After a considerable amount of coaxing, she picked up a tiny quantity of rice between her fingers, put it in her mouth, and retched. "Biliousness," I remarked. "Bring those lime pickles. Now be a good girl and finish off that rice with the help of the pickles. Go on—you can do it." She sat staring at the leaf. She took another mouthful after a good deal of persuasion and sickened. It was impossible. She rose to her feet declaring, "I can't. I won't eat any food now. I'll eat at night." She washed her hands, and went back to the hall, and lay down. I sat beside her worrying myself. She confessed: "Don't worry, it is nothing, I'll be all right."

"What is wrong?"

"Shall I say?" she whispered. "Don't be angry with me. That closet, and those, oh, oh," she shuddered, "flies and other things come before me and I can't eat. And that fly which sat here," she pointed at her lip and finished the rest of the sentence with a shiver.

Three days, four, five, and six days passed and still she did not leave her bed. It was difficult for her to swallow any food or medicine, although she was doing everything in her power to forget the picture of that closet. Luckily for me, the college was closed and I could spend much of my time with the child, who looked forlorn ever since her mother took to bed. Susila lay on her bed, spread on the floor in her room. The grey, vine-patterned bed-spread, green shawl, and that girl lying with her face to the wall, hardly awake for two hours in a day—it shattered my peace.

The old cook was very unhappy. "Please call a doctor," she suggested. It hadn't seemed to me necessary; moreover my wife was definitely against showing herself to a doctor. I told the cook, "She won't allow any doctor to see her." The cook made a gesture of despair: "Oh, you young man! Is this the time to consult her wishes!" Her question stirred vague fears in me. So I asked haughtily: "What is wrong with the time? It is quite a good time, take it from me. . . ." She ignored my petulance and said: "She has been in bed for five or six days, what have you done?"

"I have given her medicine."

"That's not enough, you must ask a doctor to see her."

"I know my duty," I replied and went away. I sat by my wife and watched her. It was morning, and she looked fairly well.

"Can you take any solid food to-day?" I asked solicitously.

"No, no, some milk and gruel will do for me. . . ."

"I will call a doctor to see you," I said.

"No, no, please. I don't like doctors," she pleaded. "They press the stomach, and here and there, and it hurts. The press given by the doctor before Leela was born still pains."

"Don't be absurd. You talk like a baby." She merely looked at me. Her lips were dry. "Where is the child?" she asked. She was playing in the next house. "Bring her down. I will comb her hair and change her dress."

"Don't exert yourself."

"No, no, I can do it. If I don't, who will do it?" she asked. I went over to the next house. Leela was heaping wet sand on their front step and sticking twigs and flowers on its top. "This is our temple," she said. The god was a piece of stone embedded in the mud. She reverently prostrated herself before it. "She is the temple man," she pointed to her friend. "She does the *puja*." Her friend came up with a piece of coconut (a castor seed) and flowers (grass tufts) and offered them to me. I said to Leela: "Your mother wants you." She brightened: "Has her fever gone?" she asked, and clutched my hand and ran down with me, leaving the temple and the priest behind.

Her mother sat up. Her hair was dishevelled, and seemed to be all in a knotted mass. Her lips were dry. She still wore the saree she had put on the day she came out with me. All the same I felt joyous. She was able to sit up—after all these days. "Try and change your dress to-day," I said. She sent

out the child to fetch the coconut oil bottle and the comb
from the cupboard in the dining hall. The child returned
hugging the bottle, put it down, and ran out a second time
to bring the comb; and sat down before her mother. Susila
remarked: "The poor child looks an orphan without proper
attention." She uncoiled her hair, oiled and combed it, and
plaited it; and then said, "Bring that blue silk frock and
shirt."

"Mother, mother, I hate that blue silk. . . ."

"You mustn't keep it in the box and outgrow it. It is nice,
wear it out."

"Mother, mother."

"Which is it?" I asked.

"The one your brother sent from Hyderabad last *Deepa-
vali*," Susila replied. All my affection for my brother returned immediately. Good fellow—I remembered the bullying
he practised on me in that cart whenever we went out together, the wild claims he would make in the afternoon that
he had trained a frog (living under a stone near the well) to
come out at his call and follow him: remember him helplessly
pacing up and down the house when his wife and mother had
heated arguments over trifles, and now auditing, henpecked,
and with twelve children—a life of worry—so good of him to
have thought of me in all this stress. . . . All this flashed before my mind and I ordered: "Little one, you must learn to
obey your mother in all these matters, without a word. . . ."
The child threw a pained look at me, and went away. I heard
her opening the box in the next room—the wicker trunk in
which her clothes were kept. My wife said: "Don't be so harsh
with her, poor girl!" The child returned with the blue frock
and shirt. I took it in my hand and said: "How lovely!" The
child replied swiftly: "It is not lovely," and submitted herself to her mother's handling. Halfway through it her mother
said: "Go and get a little water in a vessel—don't drop it on
your toes. I will wash your face. . . ."

"Here!" I cried. "You mustn't touch cold water. You may

catch a cold." My wife said: "I won't catch a cold. Her face is covered with mud." The child hesitated, and then ran over to the bathroom and fetched a vessel of water and a towel. Her mother rubbed off the mud patches with a wet towel, put a vermilion dot on her forehead, powdered her cheeks, and dressed her in new clothes. Leela looked resplendent. "Am I all right father?" she asked. I took her in my arms, "You are beautiful," I cried.

My wife changed her dress, combed her hair, and ate a little food, though she said it tasted bitter. She looked refreshed. She remade her bed. I was elated. The gloom which had hung on me for these four days lifted, and I hummed a little tune to myself as I went to my room. These exertions, however, tired her, and she lay down and slept. She woke up at five in the evening, and complained of headache. I felt her pulse, and found that she had a temperature. I said, "Just wait. I will fetch the doctor."

"Yes," she agreed. "Do something and stop this headache." "I will give you some Horlicks and go," I said. I called for boiling water. Horlicks, and a spoon and tumbler, were on a small table in the hall. I made the Horlicks and took it in to her. I found her crying. This was the first day I saw her broken and crying. "Oh you are hungry!" I cried. I tried to make her drink the Horlicks, but it was at boiling point and wouldn't cool down easily. She lay with her face towards the wall and tears made a wet track all over her face. I lost my head. The cook stood by and advised: "Give her food first, she is hungry that is all, that is all."

"But this damned thing is scalding, you can't bring a thing at bearable temperature. I've half a mind to fling away this rubbish." The child had meanwhile come in and was quietly leaning against the wall and watching us. The cook was averse to seeing her there, and kept muttering: "Come away, baby," till I, trying to cool the milk with one hand, and comforting my wife with the other, shouted at her to leave the child alone. Meanwhile my wife's sobbing increased. "Control yourself, child," I said. "Take this, you will be all right." After all the drink cooled, and she drank it, and smiled at me, I felt relieved. I sat down and caressed her forehead and asked: "Do you feel all right now? I will fetch the doctor."

§

Dr. Shankar of Krishna Medical Hall had been introduced to me by Rangappa who swore by him. "The greatest physician on earth," he used to say, "easily the most successful practitioner in the town." Krishna Medical Hall was in Market Road, and it was a mile's walk from my house. I enjoyed this outing. It suddenly relieved the stress and gloom of the last few days. I met one or two people, and spent a little time in conversation on the way, purchased a packet of cigarettes and smoked. All this seemed to restore the old glow of life— its peace and tranquillity.

The doctor was away. His seat at the central table was vacant, but all around the benches and chairs were filled with patients and patients' relatives waiting for the doctor. An accountant and a clerk sat next to each other at the entrance poring over leatherbound ledgers and making entries.

"Be seated please, the doctor will be in presently," said the clerk. I felt gratified by the warmth of his welcome and the smile he bestowed on me. I sat in a chair and looked about. The walls were lined with glass shelves loaded with the panacea that drug manufacturers invent—attractive boxes, cellophane wrappings. The days of bitter drugs were gone. All medicines were good to the taste and even to see. Piles and piles of sterilized cotton in blue packing reached the ceiling. "How do these people know where they've got the things they want, and when do they take it?" I wondered. The walls were decorated with placards containing coloured pictures of beauties and beasts and skeletons and rosy cheeked children, benefited by one cellophane covered nectar or another.

From an antechamber issued voices of women and cries of children. Somewhere else a dispenser was jingling his glasses.

(78)

He came out presently, a businesslike man wearing silk trousers, in shirt-sleeves and apron. He held up a bottle wrapped in brown paper: "Who is Kesav?"

"It.is for me," said a feeble man wrapped in a shawl with a woollen muffler over his ears. The dispenser handed him the bottle with the brief remark: "Three doses before meals," and went in. This sufferer had some further question to ask, and opened his mouth to say something, but the dispenser was gone. The man clutched his bottle and looked about helplessly, turned to the clerk and asked: "Can I take buttermilk?"

"Yes," replied the clerk.

"Should I take this immediately after or a few minutes before food?"

"Say five minutes before food," replied the clerk and added: "Six annas, please." The patient put down the change with a sad look, still feeling that he hadn't received his money's worth of doctor's advice. He hesitated, looked about and said, "I would like to ask the doctor himself. . . ."

"You need not see him till you have taken this mixture for three more days. I will tell him how you are." The patient felt grateful. "Please don't forget to say that the pain on the left side still persists."

"Yes, yes," replied the clerk, who seemed to be half a doctor. He scattered advice and suggestions liberally. He even examined throats, and suggested remedies for headache.

A car stopped, and there was an agitation in the gathering. The doctor had arrived. Everybody pressed forward to receive him. He looked like a film star being mobbed by admirers. He waved his hand, smiled, and gently pressed all his admirers back to their seats.

His assistant placed some slips of papers and bottles before him and the doctor got down to work. He read out the names on the slips and bottles one by one, examined a throat here, tapped a chest there, listened in to the murmurs of hearts through a tube, and wrote prescriptions at feverish

(79)

speed. Here he whispered into an ear something private, and there pushed someone into a private room and came out wiping his hand on a towel. He might have been a great machine dispensing health, welfare and happiness. I felt a great admiration for him. At last my turn came: "What can I do for you, professor?" he asked, mechanically picking up my wrist. For some reason he always called me professor. "I'm not the patient, doctor," I said.

I explained to him my wife's symptoms. He asked a few questions, wrote down a prescription, and put it away. He passed on to the next slip and called the next in order. A man from the village stood before him and began: "Last night . . ." The doctor turned to me and asked: "Have you brought a bottle?"

"No, I didn't expect . . ." I began apologetically.

"It is all right," he said, and on my prescription made a mark, and turned to his next patient. "Last night . . ." the other began and gave a long-winded account of a pain in the back of the head, which travelled all the way down to his ankle and went up again. He might have been a witness deposing before a magistrate. The doctor tapped his back, tingled his ear, looked into the pupils of his eyes, and pinched his knee. He cracked a couple of jokes at the expense of this patient, prescribed the treatment, and disposed of him. In a quarter of an hour the smart dispenser who had swept in the prescriptions a few minutes ago, came out with a few paper-wrapped bottles and called: "Mrs. Krishna. . . ." I stood up and took my bottle, and looked at the doctor, who was busy writing. The clerk said: "It is your bottle?" and held his hand out for it. He looked at the label and read: "A third every four hours before food, and five minutes before each dose one pill. Repeat the mixture for two days and then see the doctor. Diet—rice and buttermilk. Ten annas please." I was disappointed with the mechanical, red-tape method I found here. I looked at the doctor, he was still busy. I paid down the cash, but returned to my seat. I waited for ten minutes in the hope of catching the doctor's eye. But he was far too busy.

"Doctor," I butted in.

"Half a moment, please." He finished the prescription he was writing, leaned back, and said: "Yes, got your mixture and pills?"

"Yes." Now that I had his attention I was at a loss to know what to ask. "When is this to be given?" I asked, guiltily looking at the clerk.

"Didn't he tell you?" he asked pointing at the clerk. "Yes, yes, he did," I replied hastily. I now realized the need for this red-tape arrangement—everyone wanted to ask the same set of questions.

"But what I want to know is . . . Don't you have to see the patient?"

"Oh, no, it is just malaria. I have fifty cases like this on hand, no need to see her. I'll tell you if it is necessary. You can bring her down sometime if necessary."

"But she can't move, she is rather weak. . . ."

"Put her in a *jutka* and bring her along, nothing will happen. . . . Just peep into that room and see how many persons with fever have come here. It is usually more convenient for me than calling on them." I really felt it was absurd to have ever thought of asking this great man to visit me.

"No, no, I understand," I said awkwardly.

"Really no need. She will be all right in a couple of days. She will be all right, don't worry." He smiled confidently and it cheered me.

"Diet? What can I give her?"

"Buttermilk and rice, anything you like. Don't make it too heavy." Clutching my bottle I went out.

At the door my daughter met me. "Mother is very cross, father. She won't look at me at all, but keeps her hand over her eyes and . . ."

"Oh, she will be all right. I've brought her the medicines." My wife looked at me and asked: "Why've you taken such a long time to get back?" She was still moaning with headache. "The old lady is cooking and the baby has no one to be with. . . ."

On hearing my voice the old lady came out of the kitchen. She was overjoyed to see the medicine. "I pray to the Lord of the Seven Hills that this medicine may put her on her feet again. I am longing to see her moving about the house. What food is to be given?"

"Buttermilk and rice." She threw up her hands in horror, "I have never heard of buttermilk being given for fever!"

"Never mind. The doctor knows better. The days are gone when buttermilk was dreaded," I said haughtily.

Next day I went to the doctor, reported the patient's condition, and took home the mixture and pills, and then again the next day, and the next. It was becoming difficult to make Susila swallow the pills. It agitated her poor heart so much that she felt suffocated and perspiration left her prostrate. One night she perspired so much that she lay in a faint, and could communicate only by feeble signs. I gave her something hot to drink, and nursed her, but this condition frightened me. It was two o'clock at night. Her feet were cold.

I told the doctor about it when I met him next at his dispensary. He muttered something about idiosyncrasy and declared: "But we can't stop this pill now. It is the latest anti-malarial compound; it must be effective. It's bound to depress the heart a bit, but don't worry about it. She will be very well again. Don't stop the pills on any account."

She swallowed the medicine and pills for about a week more. The temperature did not go down.

I went to the doctor's house, and begged him to visit us. He dressed and came along. "Usually it is unnecessary. All these cases are alike. But I'll do it for your sake, professor. . . ." He drove down with me by his side to our house. He was most amiable and leisurely—an entirely different man outside the dispensary. He played with my child and gave her a ride on his shoulder, examined all the books on my table, proved to be a great book-lover and student of philosophy, and was delighted that we had similar tastes. He was over-joyed to hear that I also wrote. He had great reverence, he said, for authors as a class. He appreciated one or two pictures I'd hung on the wall. All this established such a harmony between us that when he came to examine my wife he seemed an old friend rather than the medical automaton of Krishna Dispensary.

He took half an hour to examine the patient and declared at the end of it: "Nothing to worry about. . . ."

My wife asked him: "When can I move about again?"

"Very soon. But all your life you will be moving about the house doing this and that, why should you grumble at staying a little while in bed now? Many people take it as an opportunity for a holiday. . . ." He then narrated his experience at a house, (he'd not mention names) where a daughter-in-law fell ill and was in bed for two weeks or so, and put on weight. Her husband came to him privately and said: "Doctor, please keep her in bed for a fortnight more. It is almost her only chance of being free from the harassment of her mother-in-law." On hearing this story Susila laughed so much that her face became red and she broke into sweat. He counted her pulse and said: "She is already shaking off her temperature. . . . That is a good sign. She will be absolutely well again, in a couple of days unless she wishes to stay in bed like that daughter-in-law," and he winked at me. "Take the medicine and pills, madam," he said and went away. He radiated health and cheer. Susila and I felt more confident and happy after this visit. So that when the child came from the next house she asked: "Is mother all right?"

The doctor's presence was so beneficial that I requested him to visit her at least once a day. He was very obliging; it was quite a thrill for us to hear the sound of his car every day. We gave him coffee and he stayed for over half an hour talking to us on various matters. In the evening I went to his shop to fetch the medicine. It went on for nearly a week

(83)

more. Although his visit cheered us it did not help the temperature to go down. It remained unaffected by all the drugs so far administered.

One afternoon the doctor came in, removed his coat briskly, opened his bag, and took out his sterilizer, a syringe and other things. We had never seen him getting down to business in this manner before. "Will you allow me to take just a little blood, please?" he asked. At this my wife started crying. I pacified her.

"It won't hurt, I assure you," said the doctor. "Give me a little blood and I will see what sort of fellow the mischief maker is and throw him out. . . ."

"That's good, good," he said, drawing up and sealing. "Now we will know what stick to beat him with. . . ."

I was asked to see him next morning at his dispensary. All night I kept awake. "What is the blood test going to reveal?" I kept asking myself over and over again. My wife asked: "Why is he taking the blood? Anything serious?"

"Don't be absurd, it is nothing more than malaria. He has taken it only to see what kind of malaria it is. Anyway, why do you worry? He is a good doctor, he will cure you whatever it may be. . . ."

I sat next to the doctor at his dispensary. He passed me a brown piece of paper with the stamp of the Government Hospital on it. "I sent the blood for clinical test. This is the report." I looked at the brown sheet. "Widol test positive—Typhoid. . . ." My throat went dry on reading it. "Doctor, doctor . . ." I cried. He was once again in his official seat, and so was an automaton. He said merely: "Don't worry. It is a mild attack. Take home a tin of glucose, barley and a bottle of Lentol—it is a good disinfectant. . . . I will drop in on my way home in the afternoon." I blabbered questions. He merely said: "Don't get so nervous. I attend a dozen typhoid cases every day: nothing to worry. Here, give this gentleman . . ." he gave directions to the dispenser and passed on to other patients.

(84)

I entered my house clutching a tin of glucose, some barley, a bottle of Lentol, and broke the news. I said with affected cheerfulness: "It is a very mild attack; perhaps it is only paratyphoid. If it is, you will be up and doing again in two days." She merely replied: "Keep the child away. Write to my father. You must also take something to protect yourself. . . ."

The doctor came at midday. He seemed cheered that it was typhoid. He beamed on all of us and joked continuously. "I like typhoid," he said. "It is the one fever which goes strictly by its own convention and rules. It follows a time-table and shows a great regard for those who understand its ways! Don't look so miserable, lady. Like a good daughter-in-law, make up your mind to make the most of your stay in bed for the next few weeks. . . ." Ever since she heard the word typhoid, Susila had become very silent. It was heart-rending to see her in this state. I tried to speak to her and put a little courage into her, but it was a futile effort. She lay listening to my words with grim unresponsiveness. She felt now that the doctor deserved a remark and muttered: "I thought it was malaria. . . ." "Malaria!" the doctor said. "I was only dreading lest it should be malaria—the most erratic and temperamental thing on earth. I wouldn't trust it. But typhoid is the king among fevers—it is an aristocrat who observes the rules of the game. I'd rather trust a cobra than a green snake; you can depend upon the cobra to go its way if you understand its habits and moods. . . ."

My wife's little room was converted into a sick ward.

All the furniture and odds and ends in the room were removed to the hall, where they were dumped in a heap on the floor. I had the room neatly swept. I dragged in an old wooden cot which had been put away somewhere and spread on it the thickest mattress and bed clothes, neatly folded the shawl and kept it at the foot of the bed. I fetched a small table which I used for writing and put it in a corner of the room, spread a white cloth on it and arranged all the bottles and tins on it—the yellow label of the glucose tin, the green of the barley, the pleasing violet-coloured label of Lentol—they were ranged artistically and formed a striking pattern. I looked about me proudly. The doctor nodded his head with approval. And then I brought in another stool and put on it a basin of water with a few drops of Lentol in it. It became a whitish solution and imparted a hospital aroma to the whole house. "Whenever you touch the patient or her clothes you must dip your hand in it, the best disinfectant on the market. . . ." There was a slight twinge at my heart at the new designation my wife was given: "patient". She would no longer be known as a wife or mother or Susila, but only as a patient! And all this precaution—was she an untouchable? It was a painful line of thinking, but I curbed it by much scientific argument within myself.

Now I gently lifted her and helped her to reach her new bed. "See how nice," I said with great pride. "You will come out of it with a new life. . . . All your old ailments will be gone. Even the pain at the waist you have been complaining of for so many days . . ." The doctor was tremendously pleased with the arrangement: "It is the most attractive sickroom I've ever come across. You won't get this comfort even in a special ward. . . ." I brought in a chair, put it beside the cot, and said: "See, this is where I shall be rooted."

"Plenty of glucose, barley water and mixture. (And gentle lady, don't ask for lime pickles please.) Temperature once in four hours, and note it down somewhere. . . . It'll be nice to put up a chart on the wall—you have made it look so perfectly like a special ward. . . ." I seized on this suggestion with fervour and brought out a piece of paper, and stuck it on the wall. I marked the date on it and her name. There was a morbid pleasure in this thoroughness. . . . We were setting the stage for a royal illness from which she was going to emerge fresher, stronger. . . .

The doctor said before he left: "If my reckoning is correct she is running her second week. So you have to spend less time in bed than you've already done." It was an exhilarating revelation. I stretched my mind further and further back in order to know if she had been ill longer than we counted.

"For practical purposes let us count it from the day I attended—it leaves us with an outside limit of eleven or twelve days . . ." said the doctor.

"No, doctor, it can't be so much . . ." I pleaded. I wanted it to be all my own way. The doctor ignored me and said: "I will see that her fever comes down in eleven days, and it is up to you to see that she doesn't have a relapse. . . ."

"Oh, I will take great care. You may depend upon us. . . ."

§

The following were days of iron routine. I had very little sleep all night. I got up at six o'clock in the morning and took her temperature. It was recorded once in four hours— starting with six a.m. and ending with ten at night. It duly recorded 102 at the first count. As the day progressed the mercury column rose step by step till it reached and passed 104. I watched the mercury column with a beating heart. . . . When I pulled the thermometer out of its shining case, it was always with a fine hope that the fever was going to be mild. When I stuck it under her tongue and waited, it was like waiting for a verdict—with prayer and trembling. And then taking it against the light and straining to catch its growth from 102 and 104 and the fractions it touched! I began to dread this instrument—it had something irrevocable, stern, like a judge on the bench. I always commented to myself: "Something wrong with this thermometer. Must break it and get another one." My wife asked: "What does it show?" And she was always told a degree or two less. And then the entry on the chart. When I had nothing else to do I watched the total entries on this chart, always ranging between 102 and 104. My vision of a paradise was where all the entries would be confined between normal and 100.

This was a world by itself—this sickroom. The aspirations in this chamber were of a novel kind, different from what they were outside. The chief ambition here was to see a fall in the chart. The height of contentment was reached in observing perfect bodily functions, which at other times would pass unnoticed. "The patient is hungry!" Ah, very good. "The patient likes her food." "Excellent. . . ." "The patient gives sensible answers." Marvellous. And so on and on. The depth of misery was touched when there was any deviation from these standards. The doctor came in twice a day and radiated good cheer: "Absolutely normal course. No complications. A perfect typhoid run . . ." he used to declare, make a few routine observations, and go away. I sat in that chair watching her sleep, every hour or so pouring into her throat medicine or barley water or glucose. I hardly stirred from the place, and got up only at nine in the evening when my father-in-law or mother-in-law (both of whom had arrived a few days before) took charge of the patient. After ablutions with Lentol, I went in, bathed, changed, and ate my dinner, and took charge of the child, who would not go to bed till she had me to sleep by her side in a corner of the hall.

The child exhibited model behaviour. She came and stood twice or thrice in the course of a day outside the threshold and watched her mother. Susila's eyes lit up when the child came to the door. She would ask if the little one had had her food, and put to her numerous other questions in her feeble voice, to none of which the child would reply. A sort of shyness had seized her. She conducted herself before her mother as if she were a stranger. But though she would speak no word, she liked to stand there and watch. She occasionally put a foot into the room and felt thrilled, as if it were an adventure. She went away and her mother shut her eyes and listened to her footfalls. The child spent all her time with her grandparents and her friend next door. Her grandfather took her out shopping and bought her sweets and toys. At night she waited for me to get free of sickroom duties. The moment I had sufficiently cleansed myself and warded off the poison, she hugged and clung to me, sat on my lap while I ate my dinner, and prattled away about all her day's activities. From the corner where I lay at night, I watched the sickroom, its shaded light, the low voices asking or answering; every time there was a movement in that room I woke up with a start. Once or twice when she snored, I got into a panic and ran to her door, only to see her sleeping peacefully with one of her parents sitting up in the chair.

§

My parents were unable to come. My father was down with his annual rheumatic attack, and my mother was unable to leave his side. They wrote me frantic letters every day, and it was my duty to drop them a card every day. I wrote a number of cards to others too. My brother at Hyderabad, my sister at Vellore, and the other sister at Delhi, wrote me very encouraging letters, and expected me to drop them postcards every day. They wrote, "Nothing to fear in typhoid. It is only a question of nursing." Everybody who met me repeated this like a formula, till I began to listen to it mechanically without following its meaning. Numerous people—my friends and colleagues—dropped in all day, some standing aloof fearing infection, and some coming quite close reckless and indifferent.

I lost touch with the calendar. In doing the same set of things in the same place, I lost count of days. Hours flew with rapidity. The mixture once in three hours, food every two hours, but two hours and three hours passed with such rapidity that you never felt there was any appreciable gap between doses.

But I liked it immensely. It kept me so close to my wife that it produced an immense satisfaction in my mind. Throughout I acted as her nurse. This sickness seemed to bind us together more strongly than ever. I sat in the chair and spoke to her of interesting things I saw in the paper. She spoke in whispers

(89)

as the weeks advanced. She said: "My father said he would give me five hundred rupees when I got well again. . . ."

"Very good, very good. Hurry up and claim your reward."

"Even without it I want to be well again." There was a deep stillness reigning in the house but for the voice of the child as she argued with her grandparents or sang to herself.

There was an interlude. The contractor and Sastri knocked on my door one day. "Oh, come in," I said and took them to my room, but there was no chair or table there. I said apologetically: "No chair. It is in the other room and also the table, because my wife is down with typhoid." Sastri said promptly, "Oh, we will sit on the floor." They squatted down on the floor.

And then after the preliminaries, Sastri said: "It is about that house—they are keeping it in abeyance. There is another demand for it. . . ." I remembered my decision was due long ago. "I'm afraid I can't think of it. Wait a moment please." I went up to my wife's bedside and asked: "Susila, what shall I say about that house?" She took time to understand. "Do you like it?" she asked.

"Yes, it is a fine house—if we are buying a house."

"Why not think of it when all this is over?" she said.

"Yes, yes," I agreed. I ran out and told them: "I have no time to bother about it now. If it is a loss to you waiting for me . . ." As I spoke I disliked the house. I remembered the shock Susila had received in the backyard. They went away. Before going, they said: "Nursing is everything."

"Yes, yes, I know," I said.

The contractor said: "May I say a word about it?"

"Go on, by all means."

"Never trust these English doctors. My son had typhoid. The doctors tried to give this and that and forbade him to eat anything; but he never got well though he was in bed for thirty days. Afterwards somebody gave him a herb, and I gave him whatever he wanted to eat, and he got well within two days. The last thing you must heed is their advice. The

English doctors always try to starve one to death. Give the patient plenty of things to eat and any fever will go down. That is my principle. . . ."

§

Susila's parents suffered quietly. There was a deep attachment between them and their daughter. My mother-in-law was brought up in a social condition where she had to show extreme respect for a son-in-law, and so she never came before me or spoke to me. My father-in-law was more sociable. He was an important landholder in his village, and beside that, he was on the directorate of a number of industrial concerns in Madras. He constantly travelled to and fro and met numerous people and had a very cosmopolitan outlook. So in spite of his age—he was past sixty, (my wife being his last issue)—he was rather unorthodox in his speech and habits. He constantly admonished me to be careful not to have a large family: "One grandchild from this quarter is quite adequate. We are quite satisfied." He was an extraordinarily merry person for his age. But now he looked intimidated. He was full of anxiety for his daughter's welfare and recovery, but he concealed it under a mask of light-heartedness, for fear that it might frighten me. He sat up with his daughter all night, reading a novel and speaking to her very kindly, but without betraying any excessive sentimentality in his voice. "Don't trouble me, Susila. The world is a bad enough place without your adding to it by refusing the medicine." He told me: "Your mother-in-law is definite that if you hadn't allowed her to go into that lavatory, Susila would not have fallen ill."

All day he spent unobtrusively in the company of his granddaughter, teaching her lessons, telling her stories, or taking her out shopping. He spoilt her a great deal: "I believe in spoiling children; who should be spoilt if not children?" he often asked. He undid in a couple of weeks all the elaborate cultivation of character which we imagined we had

(91)

been practising on the child for over three years now. As a result of his handling Leela spoke like an infant-in-arms (if it could speak) and constantly insisted upon being carried on her grandfather's shoulder, or grandmother's arm. Her grandmother gave her plenty to eat defeating all our regulated dieting. And I was not in a position to protest very effectively.

She was convinced that the Evil Eye had fallen on her daughter and that at the new house a malignant spirit had attacked her. She admonished me: "You should never step into an unknown house in this manner. You can never be sure. How do you know what happened to the previous tenants or why they left?" She went out in the evening and visited a nearby temple and prayed to the god for her daughter's recovery. She brought in regularly every evening sacred ash and vermilion and smeared it on her daughter's forehead. She helped us run the house and got on well with the cook, who found her a willing help. All through the day, one heard their low voices going on in the kitchen, narrating each other's life and philosophy. My mother-in-law arranged with the help of the cook for an exorcist to visit us. One fine afternoon a man came and knocked on the door. My daughter was the first to see him. My father-in-law was having his afternoon nap in my room, and my mother-in-law was in the kitchen. The little girl had been playing on the front veranda with a doll when she looked up and saw a stranger entering the gate. She let out a cry of fear on seeing him, and she came running in and stood in the doorway of the sickroom, bubbling with excitement. I was just caressing the patient's forehead, because it was the hour when the temperature mounted and she complained of headache.

"What is it, Leela?"

"There is a bad man, a fearful man there!"

I rose and followed her. I saw a man with his forehead ablaze with sacred ash, and a thick rosary around his neck and matted hair, standing at the door. "Go away," I said, taking him to be a beggar.

"I am not come to beg," he said. "I have been asked to come."

Meanwhile my mother-in-law came out, saw him, and with great respect brought him in. "He's come for Susila," she said, and conducted him to the bedside. He sat in the chair and watched the patient, while Susila who had never seen a bearded man at close quarters gazed on him in panic. Her mother said: "This *Swamiji* has come for your sake." I watched it all from the doorway in fury, but I had to be silent because I couldn't argue with my mother-in-law, and I was uncertain how it would be viewed by the *Swamiji*. He felt her pulse. He uttered some *mantras* with closed eyes, took a pinch of sacred ash and rubbed it on her forehead, and tied to her arm a talisman strung in yellow thread. When he came out of the room, my mother-in-law seated him on a mat in the hall, gave him a tumbler of milk to drink and placed before him a tray containing a coconut, betel leaves, and a rupee. Meanwhile, the doctor's car stopped before the house, and I heard his steps approaching. I felt ashamed and wished I could spirit away this mystic. The doctor came in, and saw him and smiled to himself. The mystic sat without noticing him, though looking at him. "My mother-in-law's idea of treatment," I said apologetically. "Ah, no, don't belittle these people," said the doctor. "There is a lot in him too, we don't know. When we understand it fully I am sure we doctors will be able to give more complete cures." He said this with a wink at me. My mother-in-law was greatly pleased and said to the doctor: "You must allow us old people to have our way now and then." As I went in with the doctor, the *Swamiji* got up and took his leave, muttering: "May God help you to see the end of your anxieties."

The doctor stood at the bedside. He lifted her arm, saw the talisman, and said: "Now how do you feel after this, lady?" My wife made an effort to, smile. She indicated her abdomen and said, "A lot of pain here." The doctor pressed his fingers on it. He went over to the temperature chart and scrutinized it: "You haven't taken the four o'clock temperature yet?" he said.

"No." He inserted the thermometer, took it out, and washed it. "How much?" my father-in-law asked, standing at the door, having been disturbed out of his nap by the visitors. "The usual run," the doctor answered. My father-in-law asked one or two questions about the patient and moved on. The doctor closely observed the patient and her movements and left the room. I followed him to his car, listening to instructions. At the car he told me, "Have you an ice bag?"

"No."

"I will send one. Get some ice and apply it constantly, whenever the temperature is above 102."

"What is the temperature, doctor?"

"Rather high to-day, but don't get into a fright. 105, but that is common in this fever. Apply ice." He went away.

All day I sat pressing down the ice bag on her forehead. The Bombay Ananda Bhavan, where we had our morning tiffin on that Sunday, and perhaps where she had caught her typhoid, had a refrigerator and sold us ice. I purchased a block of ten pounds at a time, covered with sawdust and wrapped in gunny. My father-in-law obliged me by keeping an eye on the ice position and going out and getting it. I loved the smooth crystal appearance as I opened the gunny sack covering and wiped away the sawdust particles; the cool gust which emanated from it; and then the hammer blow which split it up into lumps just the size to be put into the ice bag. I always took a pride in the fact that the blow I gave was so well calculated that the pieces were neither too large nor too small but of the correct size and slipped into the mouth of the bag. . . . It was a queer delight for me to see the bag bulging, I liked the feel of it as it acquired the correct weight. I carried it in, sat down, with a towel in hand, and pressed it down to form a cap on her head; when it fitted her head nicely it gave me a profound satisfaction. I sat pressing it down with one hand, while with the towel I wiped off the trickling drops of water condensing on it. My palm froze by this constant contact with ice and her forehead felt like a marble surface on a winter morning. And as the ice inside melted, it made a peculiar gurgling when the bag was shaken, so that by practice and intuition I learnt to gauge how much of the ice inside had melted, without opening the lid. Everything in this sickroom seemed to me profoundly ingenious and full of technical points and pleasures and triumphs. This impressed me so much that one day I wrote a poem about it. With my left hand I was applying the ice on her forehead. She slept and spoke a little in her sleep; I watched her for a while; a coloured bee had drifted in and was droning near the rafters. I had nothing else to do. I left the ice bag balanced on her head, ran in and returned with my writing pad and a pencil. I placed the pad on my lap and wrote, while she slept and talked in sleep:

> The Great Kaïlas is one Mound of Ice
> Where Shiva and Parvathi sport, which catch the
>   Gleam of ethereal lights, heavenly Rainbows.
> Here for us God has sent a piece of Kailas down
>   To subdue the Mercury column. . . .
> And here out of its wood dust it comes,
>   Cold mist cloud rises on its crystal face,
> And it reflects not mountain light
>   But my face. . . .
>
> And here it is a great battle ground,
>   The great fight goes on
> On either side of this red bag.
>   But so far it is not the fever which cools,
> But Ice that melts.

It was a fact. Ice turned into water with great rapidity. I had to hammer out blocks into pieces every twenty minutes. It was not necessary to keep the ice on at night, but in a couple of days it became indispensable even then. The temperature declined only after midnight. She spoke less clearly now, took time to understand what was being said to her, and she constantly agitated her arms up and down. "Why do you do it?" I asked.

"Something is running up and down. I won't sleep here unless you make a new bed." With elaborate difficulty, my father-in-law, mother-in-law and everybody assisting, we rolled her to one side and made a new bed for her. It took us nearly an hour. Changing the sheets was a daily adventure, but now we had to make an entirely new bed for her top to bottom. But the labour was worth it, because she remained quiet, but only for an hour. Again she began to toss her arms and legs. "You can't do it, child," I said. "You will put up your fever." She merely glared at me and said: "Don't tell me all that. I know how to look after myself." I sat down and applied the ice. She tried to seize the ice bag and push it away. "Oh, I don't want this, please. I am tired of it." I had to cajole and admonish and keep the bag. She went on grumbling and muttering something. I had to beg her to keep quiet: and when she persisted, I called in her father.

"Do you think I am a child to be frightened?" she asked when her father stood in the doorway.

"Come in, come in, please," I said to her father. He came over and stood at her bedside. She said: "Father!" She implored weakly, "He is worrying me too much. I don't want the ice bag."

"All right, all right, child, it is good for you. I will apply it." He sat down in the chair. He took up the ice bag and said to me: "Why don't you go to your room and rest for a while? It will do you good. You have been sitting up without a break since 6 a.m. I will look after her."

"No, it will be a bother for you. Not your hour. You'll have to sit up at night too."

"Oh, it doesn't matter. I do not really mind a little overtime work," he said. I dipped my hand in Lentol and left the room.

The child was delighted to see me out of the room so early. She clapped her hands in joy and ran towards me. "Not yet, not yet. Don't touch me. You can speak to me from a distance, that is all. I have not had a wash yet. I'll have it only at night." She made a wry face: "All right. I'll go to grandfather."

"He is with mother."

She became angry on hearing this. "Everybody goes into that room. Who is to be with me?"

"Why don't you go to the next house and play with your friend?"

"I don't like her. She beats me whenever she sees me." This amused me. I knew they were the thickest of friends a second ago. And they would be playing together next minute. So I asked: "All right, then. Come to my room and see a picture book. You must not sit on my bed but a little way off."

She agreed to this condition and came to my room. My room served as a guest room for my father-in-law. In a corner there was his canvas hold-all and a trunk, and his coats and clothes hung on the peg. My table was dusty and confused, the books lying in a chaotic jumble, untouched for days and days now. All my waking hours were spent at the bedside, and I seldom visited this room. "In my happy days this table was a jumble. In my days of anxiety it was no less a jumble. Perhaps a table is meant to be so. No use wasting thought over it . . ." I remarked to myself; the habit of wishing to do something or other with the table top, whenever I saw it, had persisted with me for many years now. I kicked up a roll of matting and threw myself down, deciding to relax while the chance was there. "Let the father and daughter settle it between themselves. I won't go till I am called." My daughter, who had been standing in the doorway, asked: "Can I come in, father?"

"Yes, yes, this is not a sickroom," I said. I had forgotten for a moment I had asked her to follow me in.

She sat down on the edge of the mat, and asked: "Is this far enough?"

"Yes, you mustn't touch me, that is all, till I have a thorough wash at night."

"Does mother's fever climb on your hands and stick there?"

"Yes."

"Won't it get into you?"

"No."

"Why?"

"Because I am an elder," I said with a touch of pride in my voice. She was gradually edging nearer to my mat, and now only an inch of space separated us. "No, no. You are too near me," I said.

"I'm not touching you," she argued. I was too fatigued to argue with her, and left her alone, turned over to the other side, and shut my eyes, muttering: "You are a fine girl. Don't disturb me. I am sleeping." She agreed to this proposal. But the moment I shut my eyes, she stretched her leg and gently poked my back with her toe.

"Ah, why do you do it?"

"You must not turn away from me. It makes me afraid to be alone." I turned over to face her and tried to sleep. She called: "Father."

"You mustn't disturb me."

"You said you would give me a picture book." I groaned, "Leave me alone, baby. Take the book." She went over to the table, but could not reach any part of its top. "It is too high up, father." I got up and searched among the books on the table. There was not one fit for her perusal—all of them were heavy, academic, and unillustrated. Underneath all these was a catalogue of miscellaneous articles from a mail order firm in Calcutta. It was a stout enough volume. I gave it to her. She was delighted. It was full of small smudgy representations of all kinds of household articles. She kept it on her knees and was soon lost in it, turning the pages. Soothed by the rustling of the pages, I snatched a little sleep, although she constantly tried to get me to explain the pictures.

When I woke up it was about five o'clock. The catalogue was sprawling on the floor. The child was not there. Her voice came from the kitchen. I went in and asked for some coffee. The child was sitting there on her grandmother's lap, learning a song. On seeing me she stopped her song and asked: "Can I touch you now?"

"Not yet."

"You didn't know it when I got up and ran away!" she said with a great triumph in her voice, as if I had kept her in detention and she had managed to escape.

"No, I didn't. You are very cunning," I replied and it pleased her greatly.

The patient was asleep. My father-in-law rose from his seat on seeing me, dipped his hand in the basin, and came out and whispered: "Will you take the watch now?"

"Yes."

"She has managed to sleep after all. Let her sleep quietly. Rather restless to-day . . ." he said and went away.

I resumed my seat, pressing down the ice bag. She woke up. She looked up at me and said: "Oh, you have come!" She gripped my arms gratefully.

"I am always here. Don't worry, dear."

"Yes, yes, I'm glad. Do you know what that man did?"

"Who?" I said.

"He was here when you were away."

"Your father?" I said.

"Know what he did? He tried to remove this necklace," she lifted her gold neckchain between her fingers and showed it to me. "But I snatched it back. He wrenched my hand. Bad man. You must never leave my side hereafter."

I agreed. Her fingers lightly ran over the bedclothes as if searching for something, and tugged the edges. She tried to kick away the blanket. She attempted to roll out of bed.

(99)

When I checked her, she was furious. "Why do you stop me? I want to go away."

She held up her arms and asked: "Where is the baby?"

"In the kitchen," I explained.

"Oh, who took her there?"

"Your mother," I said.

"All right. Let them be careful. They must not take away a small baby without telling me. They may drop it." I understood what she meant. She was imagining herself in childbed. Those memories were confusing her. She still held up her arms for the baby. I gently put them down. After that she started singing. Her faint voice choked with the strain. I couldn't make out the words or the tune. I said: "Hush, stop it please. You must not sing. You will not get well if you exert yourself." But she would not stop. I protested, and she said: "I want to sing, and I will sing. Why should it offend you?"

At night she ceased to sleep peacefully. She talked or sang all night. The doctor examined her more closely every time now. He examined her heart and said: "She must sleep. It is imperative. This continuous temperature is very taxing. She must rest. I will watch how it goes, and then give a mild hypnotic."

The ice was melting, we were wearing ourselves out nursing, but the fever would not subside. It never went below 103 in the mornings and rose and hovered about 105 every day. The doctor said: "The patient is very restless, that's why she has a temperature. If only she could sleep for six hours, you would see a wonderful change."

The doctor was losing his cheerfulness, and looked harrowed and helpless. Next morning he brought in his car another doctor, a famous Madras physician. Even in our wildest dreams we could never have hoped to get this great physician. His reputation was all over the Presidency and his monthly income was in the neighbourhood of ten thousand. Dr. Sankar came in advance and said: "It's your luck, Doctor

——— came here for another case. I begged him to see your wife. You are lucky he has agreed. Please ask him in. He is a very good man." I and my father-in-law rushed out and greeted the great physician effusively, opened the door of the car, and led him in. Dr. Sankar looked very nervous in his presence.

The great man spent an hour examining the patient. He tapped her abdomen, scratched a key on it and watched, lifted her arm, flashed a torch into her eyes, and examined the temperature chart. We waited in great suspense. He asked numerous questions. "Mixture?" he said and held his hand out for it without turning. Dr. Sankar jumped up, clutched the medicine bottle, and put it in his hand. The great doctor shook the contents and watched it for a moment: "If I were you, I'd stop all this and go so far as to administer glucose and brandy every two hours, if possible with five minims of solomine. It is the best stimulant I can think of at the moment."

"How do you find the patient, sir?" I asked.

"Well . . ." the expert drawled. "Her vitality is not very good, though there are no complications."

"What can we do? What can we do?" my father-in-law asked in consternation. My mother-in-law stood in the doorway, and behind her the child, looking with wonder on this scene. The doctor did not answer. But my father-in-law writhed: "Is there anything wanting in our attention? Should we take her to the hospital?"

"Not at all. Everything is quite well done here," said the physician and we were greatly pleased with the compliment. "Is there anything special we ought to do now?"

"I will speak to your doctor," said the big man, with an air of snubbing us.

We poured out our gratitude as he moved to his car, and asked: "Won't you have a cup of coffee?"

"Thank you, I never drink coffee," he said.

Our doctor said: "I'll see you again," and went away.

(101)

The next morning I was jubilant. For the first time the temperature remained at 101. For weeks it had never gone below 102. Now it showed 101. What a joy! We were all jubilant. A ray of sun was breaking through the overcast sky. As soon as our doctor's car drove up at our gate, I ran out to announce, "Doctor, the temperature has come down."

"Splendid," he cried. "Didn't I tell you it would. . . ."

"And the patient slept grandly," I said. "In fact she is still sleeping. . . ."

The doctor examined her, but it didn't wake her up. "Continue the mixture, and diet as usual. No ice bag. . . . Have a hot water bottle ready. I will come again," he said and went away. For the first time these weeks my hand did not have to perform the duty of pressing down the ice bag. It lay on a stool untouched. It was a happy sight for me. And also there were still five pounds of ice in the sack. "Use it for ice cream, if you like," I told my father-in-law. The atmosphere had suddenly relaxed. The patient had gone into a profound sleep. I had nothing to do in the sickroom. I sat there till afternoon. I disinfected my hands and requested my father-in-law to keep an eye on the patient. I bathed, changed, and took the child upon my shoulder. She was astonished: "Has mother got well?" she asked. "Can I go in now?"

"Very soon you will be going in . . . but wait. I will take you out for a walk. . . ." She was elated. She put on her small green coat, clung to my hand and came out. I took her down the road. Her friend was standing at the gate. Leela said: "Let her also come with us, father. She is so poor!"

"Is she very poor?"

"Yes."

"What is meant by poor?" I asked.

"Nobody buys her peppermints . . ." the child exclaimed.

"Who taught you this?"

"Grandmother," she replied promptly. So her friend joined us. We then paced down the road. They didn't speak much, but constantly looked at eath other and giggled. I took them to a shop at the end of the street, and allowed them to buy whatever they wanted. They chose a few lozenges, and some bright bamboo whistles pasted over with green coloured paper. We returned, both of them blowing through their whistles. All this had taken about an hour, and I had lived in a great peace. Ahead, at our gate I saw the doctor's car standing. "Let us hurry up," I said walking fast, and the children trotted behind. At our door the child said: "I will go and play in the next house, father," and ran off. I went in. The doctor and my father-in-law were in earnest discussion; the patient was sleeping, breathing noisily.

"The child, the child," the old man said in a shaking voice the moment he saw me. "Where is she?"

I didn't understand. "She has gone to play in the next house," I said.

"Very well, very well," he replied. "Take care of her. You must mind her and keep her."

I looked at the patient. She had grown a shade whiter, and breathed noisily. There were drops of perspiration on her forehead. I touched it, and found it very cold. "Doctor, the temperature is coming down."

"Yes, yes, I knew it would . . ." he said, biting his nails. Nothing seemed to be right anywhere. "Doctor . . . tell me. . . ."

"For heaven's sake, don't ask questions," he said. He felt the pulse; drew aside the blanket and ran his fingers over her abdomen which appeared slightly distended. He tapped it gently, and said: "Run to the car and fetch the other bag please, which you will find in the back seat. . . ."

The doctor opened it. "Hot water, hot water, please." He poured turpentine into the boiling water, and applied fomentations to her abdomen. He took out a hypodermic syringe, heated the needle, and pushed it into her arm: at the pressure of the needle she winced. "Perhaps it hurts her," I muttered. The doctor looked at me without an answer. He continued the fomentation.

An hour later, he drew up the blanket and packed his bag. I stood and watched in silence. All through this, he wouldn't speak a word to me. I stood like a statue. The only movement the patient showed was the heaving of her bosom. The whole house was silent. The doctor held his bag in one hand, patted my back and pursed his lips. My throat had gone dry and smarted. I croaked through this dryness: "Don't you have to remain, doctor?" He shook his head: "What can we do? We have done our best. . . ." He stood looking at the floor for a few moments, heaved a sigh, patted my back once again, and whispered: "You may expect a change in about two and a half hours." He turned and walked off. I stood stock still, listening to his shoe creaks going away, the starting of his car; after the car had gone, a stony silence closed in on the house, punctuated by the stentorian breathing, which appeared to me the creaking of the hinges of a prison gate, opening at the command of a soul going into freedom.

§

Here is an extract from my diary: The child has been cajoled to sleep in the next house. The cook has been sent there to keep her company. Two hours past midnight. We have all exhausted ourselves, so a deep quiet has descended on us (moreover a great restraint is being observed by all of us for the sake of the child in the next house, whom we don't wish to scare). Susila lies there under the window, laid out on the floor. For there is the law that, the body, even if it is an Emperor's must rest only on the floor, on Mother Earth.

We squat on the bare floor around her, her father, mother, and I. We mutter, talk among ourselves, and wail between convulsions of grief; but our bodies are worn out with fatigue. An unearthly chill makes our teeth chatter as we gaze on the inert form and talk about it. Gradually, unknown to ourselves, we recline against the wall and sink into sleep. The dawn finds us all huddled on the cold floor.

The first thing we do is to send for the priests and the bearers. . . . And then the child's voice is heard in the next house. She is persuaded to have her milk there, dress, and go out with a boy in the house, who promises to keep her engaged and out of our way for at least four hours. She is surprised at the extraordinary enthusiasm with which people are sending her out to-day. I catch a glimpse of her as she passes on the road in front of our house, wearing her green velvet coat, bright and sparkling.

Neighbours, relations and friends arrive, tears and lamentations, more tears and lamentations, and more and more of it. The priest roams over the house, asking for one thing or other for performing the rites. . . . The corpse-bearers, grim and sub-human, have arrived with their equipment—bamboo and coir ropes. Near the front step they raise a small fire with cinders and faggots—this is the fire which is to follow us to the cremation ground.

A bamboo stretcher is ready on the ground in front of the house. Some friends are hanging about with red eyes. I am blind, dumb, and dazed.

The parting moment has come. The bearers, after brief and curt preliminaries, walk in, lift her casually without fuss, as if she were an empty sack or a box, lay her on the stretcher, and tie her up with ropes. Her face looks at the sky, bright with the saffron touched on her face, and the vermilion on the forehead, and a string of jasmine somewhere about her head.

The downward curve of her lips gives her face a repressed smile. . . . Everyone gathers a handful of rice and puts it between her lips—our last offering.

They shoulder the stretcher. I'm given a pot containing the fire and we march out, down our street, Ellamman Street. Passers-by stand and look for a while. But every face looks blurred to me. The heat of the sun is intense. We cut across the sands, ford the river at Nallappa's Grove, and on to the other bank of the river, and enter the cremation ground by a small door on its southern wall.

The sun is beating down mercilessly, but I don't feel it.

I feel nothing, and see nothing. All sensations are blurred and vague.

They find it necessary to put down the stretcher a couple of times on the roadside. Half a dozen flies are dotting her face. Passers-by stand and look on sadly at the smiling face. A madman living in Ellamman Street comes by, looks at her face and breaks down, and follows us on, muttering vile and obscure curses on fate and its ways.

Stretcher on the ground. A deep grove of tamarind trees and mangoes, full of shade and quiet—an extremely tranquil place. Two or three smouldering pyres are ranged about, and bamboos and coirs lie scattered, and another funeral group is at the other end of this grove. "This is a sort of cloak-room, a place where you leave your body behind," I reflect as we sit down and wait. Somebody appears carrying a large notebook, and writes down name, age, and disease; collects a fee, issues a receipt, and goes away.

The half a dozen flies are still having their ride. After weeks, I see her face in daylight, in the open, and note the devastation of the weeks of fever—this shrivelling heat has baked her face into a peculiar tinge of pale yellow. The purple cotton saree which I bought her on another day is wound round her and going to burn with her.

The priest and the carriers are ceaselessly shouting for someone or other. Basket after basket of dry cowdung fuel is brought and dumped. . . . Lively discussion over prices and quality goes on. The trappings of trade do not leave us even here. Some hairy man sits under a tree and asks for alms. I am unable to do anything, but quietly watch in numbness. . . . I'm an imbecile, incapable of doing anything or answering any questions. I'm incapable of doing anything except what our priest orders me to do. Presently I go over, plunge in the river, return, and perform a great many rites and mutter a lot of things which the priest asks me to repeat.

They build up a pyre, place her on it, cover her up with layers of fuel. . . . Leaving only the face and a part of her chest out, four layers deep down. I pour ghee on and drop the fire.

We are on our homeward march, a silent and benumbed gang. As we cross Nallappa's Grove once again, I cannot resist the impulse to turn and look back. Flames appear over the wall. . . . It leaves a curiously dull pain at heart. There are no more surprises and shocks in life, so that I watch the flame without agitation. For me the greatest reality is this and nothing else. . . . Nothing else will worry or interest me in life hereafter.

CHAPTER FOUR

THE DAYS had acquired a peculiar blankness and emptiness.
The only relief was my child, spick and span and fresh, and
mocking by her very carriage the world of elders. I dared not
contemplate where I should have been but for her. So much
so that I refused to allow her to be taken away by her grandparents and decided to keep her with me. It was a wonder to
them how I was going to look after the girl—but our nature
adapts itself to circumstances with wonderful speed. In three
or four months I could give her a bath with expert hands,
braid her hair passably, and wash and look after her clothes,
and keep correct count of her jackets and skirts. I slipped
into my double role with great expertness. It kept me very
much alive to play both father and mother to her at the same
time. My one aim in life now was to see that she did not
feel the absence of her mother. To this end I concentrated
my whole being. From morning till night this kept me busy.
I had to keep her cheerful and keep myself cheerful too lest
she should feel unhappy.

My mother could come and stay with me only for a couple
of weeks occasionally, and whenever she was here, I could
well imagine what it meant to my father, who could not get
on for a day without her help. Of late he had become utterly
helpless, nearly starved, and could not look after himself even
for an hour if she was away. He did not know where his
clothes were, when to go in for dinner, or what to ask for at
dinner. When she came and stayed with me for a week or two
at a time, it took months to bring him and his health under
control again. My mother was very good and helped me

ungrudgingly. But I could not accept her service indefinitely. "God has given me some novel situations in life. I shall live it out alone, face the problems alone, never drag in another to do the job for me. . . ." I found a peculiar satisfaction in making this resolve. And next time when my mother had to leave, I did not remonstrate with her as I used to do. She suggested: "Kittu, send the child with me. Why are you so stubborn?" I was. She grew angry with me when I went to see her off. She sat in the bus. I and the little child stood by waiting for the bus to start. I made it a point to take the child wherever I went, except the college. "You are unpractical and stubborn," my mother persisted. "How are you going to look after her?" "As if it were a big feat!" I replied with bravado. "God intends me to learn these things and do them efficiently. I can't shirk it. . . ." Tears gathered in my mother's eyes. "That I should be destined to see these scenes in our life—I have never known such things in our family." I let her quietly have her cry. I was used to such situations and treated them with businesslike indifference. Condolences, words of courage, lamentations, or assurances, were all the same. I had become a sort of professional receptacle of condolence and sympathy, and I had received them in such quantity these months that they had ceased to move me or mean anything. Death and its associates, after the initial shock, produce callousness. . . .

My mother averted her face in order that the child might not observe the tears in her eyes. The child asked: "When will you be back, mother?" She controlled her voice and gave some vague reply. I didn't want the child to have any illusions about things and be misled. Living without illusions seemed to be the greatest task for me in life now. So I explained, "She can't come again for a long time, child; she has to look after grandfather. . . ." That was the stuff to give humanity, nurtured in illusions from beginning to end! The twists and turns of fate would cease to shock if we knew, and expected nothing more than, the barest truths and facts of life. The child accepted my answer with calmness. "How long will she be away?" This was a point about which I could not be very clear. But it moved my mother and she said, "I shall try to be back as soon as possible. I only wish your grandfather were more helpful."

The bus conductor blew his whistle. The driver sat on his seat. An old village woman, with a basket on her knee, sitting next to my mother asked, "Where are you going?"

"Kamalapuram. . . . My son is employed here. There you see him with his child. . . ." She whispered, "A motherless child and so I come here often." At which the village woman clapped her hands and wailed, "Oh, the poor child! Oh, the poor child!" She insisted upon having the child lifted up and shown to her. She touched the child's cheeks and cracked her fingers on her temple as an antidote for Evil Eye. She cried: "What a beauty! And a girl!" She sighed deeply, and my mother was once again affected. I wished the bus would move. But the conductor would not allow it to go, he was deeply involved in a controversy with another villager who refused to pay the regular fare but wanted some concession. . . . The village woman now said: "When is he marrying again?" I was shocked to hear it, and my mother felt confused. She knew how much such talk upset me. . . . She did not wish me to overhear it. But the old woman stared at me and said: "You must marry again, you are so young!" My mother was agitated, and desperately tried to suppress her. . . . "Oh, don't speak of all that now." The old woman could not be suppressed so easily. She said: "Why not? He is so young! How can he manage the child?"

"That is what I also say," my mother echoed indiscreetly.

"Men are spoilt if they are without a wife at home," added the old woman. I looked desperately at the conductor who showed no signs of relenting. I said: "Conductor, isn't it time to start?"

"Yes, sir, look at this man . . ."

"He wants four annas for . . ." began the controversialist.

The old woman was saying: "A man must marry within fifteen days of losing his wife. Otherwise he will be ruined. I was the fourth wife to my husband and he always married within three weeks. All the fourteen children are happy. What is wrong?" she asked in an argumentative manner. The bus roared and started and jerked forward. My daughter sat in my arms, watching the whole scene spellbound. As the bus moved my mother said: "Don't fail to give her an oil anointment and bath every Friday. Otherwise she will lose all her hair. . . ."

§

I was never a sound sleeper at any time in life, but now more than ever I lay awake most of the night, sleeping by fits and starts. My mind kept buzzing with thoughts and memories. In the darkness I often felt an echo of her voice and speech or sometimes her moaning and delirious talk in sickbed. The child lay next to me sleeping soundly. We both slept in my little study on the front veranda. The door of the room in which my wife passed away remained shut. It was opened once a week for sweeping, and then closed again and locked. This had been going on for months now. It was expected that I should leave the house and move to another. It seemed at first a most natural and inevitable thing to do. But after the initial shocks had worn out, it seemed unnecessary and then impossible. At first I put it down to a general disinclination for change and shifting. To remove that chair, and that chaotic table with its contents . . . and then another and another. . . . We had created a few favourite corners in the house, and it seemed impossible to change and settle in a new house. My daughter had played on the edge of that veranda ever since she came to me as a seven-month baby. Yes, at first I put it down to a general disinclination for change, but gradually I realized the experience of life in that house was too precious and that I wouldn't exchange it for anything. There were subtle links with a happy past; they were not merely links but blood channels, which fed the stuff of memory. . . . Even sad and harrowing memories were cherished by me; for in the contemplation of those sad scenes and hapless hours, I seemed to acquire a new peace, a new outlook; a view of life with a place for everything.

The room which was kept shut had an irresistible fascination for my daughter. She looked at the door with a great deal of puzzlement. On that unhappy day when we had returned from the cremation-ground, the child had also just come home. "Father, why is that door shut?" It threw us into a frenzy. We did not know what to reply. The house at that time was full of guests, all adults—all looking on, suffering, and bewildered by death. Death was puzzling enough, but this question we felt was a maddening conundrum. We looked at each other and stood speechless. My daughter would not allow us to rest there. She repeated authoritatively: "Why is that door closed?" My father-in-law was deeply moved by this. He tried to change her mind by asking: "Would you like to have a nice celluloid doll?"

"Yes, where is it?" she asked.

"In the shop. Let us go and buy one." She picked up her green coat, which she had just discarded, and said: "All right, let us go, grandfather." It had been a strenuous morning and we had eaten our food late in the day and were about to rest. He looked forlorn. "Come on," she said and he looked at me pathetically. I told my daughter, "You are a good girl, let your grandfather rest for a little while and then he will take you out. . . ." She said: "Why have you had your meal so late?" Another inconvenient question under which we smirked. We were all too fatigued to invent new answers to beguile her mind. She waited for a moment and returned to her original charge. "Doll—come on grandfather." He had by this time thrown himself on the floor and was half sunk in sleep. I said: "Child, you are a nice child. Allow your grandfather to rest. He will take you out and buy two dolls." She was displeased at this, removed her coat and flung it down. I couldn't check her, as I would have done at other times. She looked at me fixedly and asked: "Why is that door closed?" At which everyone was once again convulsed and confused and dismayed. She seemed to look on this with a lot of secret pleasure. She waited for an answer with ruthless determination. "Mother is being given a bath, that is why the door is closed. . . ." She accepted the explanation with a nod of her head, and then went up to her wooden trunk containing toys, rummaged and picked out a rag book. I went away to my room and reclined on my easy chair. As I closed my eyes, I heard her footfalls approaching. She thrust the rag book under my nose and demanded: "Read this story." I had read that "story" two hundred times already. The book was dirty with handling. And she always kept it with all the junk in her trunk. It had illustrations in green, and a running commentary of a couple of lines under each. It was really not a story, there was not one in it, but a series of illustrations of tiger, lion, apple, and Sam—each nothing to do with the other. But Leela would never accept the fact that they were disconnected. She maintained that the whole book was one story—and always commanded me to read it; so I fused them all into a whole and gave her a "story"—"Sam ate the apple, but the lion and tiger wanted some of it . . ." and so on. And she always listened with interest, completely accepting the version. But unfortunately I never repeated the same version and this always mystified her! "No, father, Sam didn't hit the tiger," she would correct. So when this book was pressed into my hand to-day my heart parched at the thought of having to narrate a story. . . . "Once upon a time . . ." I said, and somehow went on animating the pictures in the book with my narration. She said: "You are wrong, father, it didn't happen that way. Your story is very wrong. . . ."

Towards the evening she came up once again and asked: "The door is still closed, father. Is she bathing still?"

"H'm. If the door is open, she may catch a cold. . . ."

"Don't you have to go to her?"

"No. . . ."

"Is she all alone?"

"There is a nurse who looks after her."

"What is a nurse?"

"A person who tends sick people."

"You don't have to go and stay with mother any more, ever?"

"No, I will always be with you." She let out a yell of joy and threw herself on me.

Four days later, she stole into my room one evening, and whispered, with hardly suppressed glee: "Father, say what I have done?"

"What is it?"

"There was no one there and it wasn't locked; so I pushed the door open and went in. Mother is not there!" She shook with suppressed glee, at the thought of her own escapade.

"God, give me a sensible answer for this child," I prayed.

"Oh," I said casually and added, "the nurse must have taken her away to the hospital."

"When will she be back?"

"As soon as she is all right again." I replied.

§

The first thing that woke me in the morning was the cold hands of my daughter placed on my forehead and the shout "Appa" (father), or sometimes she just sat, with her elbows on the ground and her chin between her palms, gazing into my face as I lay asleep. Whenever I opened my eyes in the morning, I saw her face close to mine, and her eyes scrutinizing my face. I do not know what she found so fascinating there. Her eyes looked like a pair of dark butterflies dancing with independent life, at such close quarters.

"Oh, father has woken up!" she cried happily. I looked at her with suspicion and asked: "What have you been trying to do so close to me?" "I only wanted to watch, that is all. I didn't wake you up."

"Watch what?"

"I wanted to watch if any ant or fly was going to get into you through your nose, that is all. . . ."

"Did any get in?"

"No. Because I was watching." There was a hint in her tone as if a sentry had mounted guard against a formidable enemy.

"What do you do when you sleep, father?" Once again a question that could not be answered by an adult; perhaps only another child could find an answer for it. "I was saying something close to you and yet you didn't reply."

"What were you saying?"

"I said: There is a peppermint, open your mouth!"

After these preambles we left the bed. I rolled her about a little on the mattress and then she sat up and picked a book from my table and commanded: "Read this story." I had no story book on my table. She usually picked up some heavy critical work and brought it to me. When I put it back on the table, she brought out her usual catalogue of the Calcutta mail order firm, and asked me to read out of it. This happened almost every morning. I had to put away the book gently and say to her: "Not now. We must first wash."

"Why?"

"That is how it must be done."

"No. We must first read stories," she corrected me.

"We must first wash, and then read stories," I persisted.

"Why?"

"Because it is Goddess Saraswathi and we must never touch her without washing."

"What will she do if we touch her without washing?"

"She will be very unhappy, and she is the Goddess of Learning, you see, and if you please her by washing and being clean, she will make you very learned."

"Why should I be learned?"

"You can read a lot of stories yourself without my help."

"Oh! What will you do then?" she asked, as if pitying a man who would lose his only employment in life.

It was as a matter of fact my chief occupation in life. I cared for little else. I felt a thrill of pride whenever I had to work and look after the child. It seemed a noble and exciting occupation—the sole responsibility for a growing creature.

CHAPTER FIVE

THE DAY had been unusually heavy. I had more or less continuous work till three in the afternoon. And at three, when I was looking at the clock, hoping to drop things and go home, I received a note from Gajapathy to say that I was to take Fourth Hons. Class, because George of the language section was absent. Some teachers were absent this week, exhausting their leave, and those who were present were saddled with extra work. I implored Gajapathy to spare me this pain since as a student I had found language a torture, and as a teacher I still found it a torture. But he said: "Just keep the boys engaged. The Principal doesn't want to let the boys off when they have not a teacher for a particular period. In the English department everybody ought to be able to handle any part of it; and I agree with him." And I had no option but to sit down in the Fourth Hons. Class and engage their young minds in tittle-tattle for an hour. Our chief believed in keeping them well-read, and when they had spare time, in spending it over a library book of some consequence. I sent a boy to the library to fetch any book from the English section he liked. He brought down a book of nineteenth-century essays and I sat down to read mechanically through the pages aloud: the boys were busy, with a lot of conversation among themselves. In harmony with this din I read on. Some boys in the front listened. But they found it difficult to hear and complained: "Can't hear, sir."

"Ask your friends to shut up and you will hear better," I said. They turned and stared helplessly at the noise-makers behind them. It was a small class and I could have easily established law and order, but I was too weary to exert myself. I was past that stage of exertion. A terrible fatigue and inertia had come over me these days and it seemed to me all the same whether they listened or made a noise or whether they understood what I said or felt baffled, or even whether they heard it at all or not. My business was to sit in that chair and keep my tongue active—that I did. My mind itself could only vaguely comprehend what was being read. . . . "This influence became so marked towards the later part of the century that those writers seized on it with avidity. It was a new-found treasure for the literary craftsman, a new weapon for his arsenal, shall we say. . . ." My voice dully fell on my ears, but my mind refused to maintain pace with its sense. I caught myself constantly reflecting: "What is it all about? What influence? On whom? Oh, good author, why not say arsenal or whatever you like if you choose?"

Into this pandemonium the most welcome sound impinged —the college bell. It was the end of the hour and of the day. I felt like a schoolboy, genuinely happy that I could go home now to the child waiting for me there, all ready and bubbling with joy; ready to be taken out and ready with a hundred questions on her lips. . . .

I made my way into the common room, to put away the books in my locker, pick up my umbrella, and go out. As I was closing my locker, the servant came up and said: "There is someone asking for you, master." I looked out. He was a stranger, a young boy about fifteen years old. He was standing on the path below the veranda, a thin young man with a tuft behind, and wearing a small cap—a poor boy, I felt, by the look of him; out to ask for a donation for his school fee or something of the kind. "Father seriously ill, money for his medicines." One or other of the numerous sad excuses for begging. Of late they were on the increase. . . . Formerly I used to investigate and preach to them and so on, but now I felt too weary to exert myself and paid out change as far as possible. I saw his hand, bringing out an envelope, and

I put my hand in my pocket for my purse. "The usual type-written petition addressed to all whom it may concern," I said to myself.

"What is it?" I asked.

"Are you Krishna of the English section?"

"Yes."

"Here is a letter for you."

"From whom?"

"My father has sent it. . . ."

"Who is your father?"

"You'll find it all in that letter," he replied. It was a bulky envelope. I tore it open. There was a long sheet of paper, wrapped around which was a small note on which was written: "Dear Sir,

"I received this message last evening, while I was busy writing something else. I didn't understand what it meant. But the directions, address and name given in it are clear and so I have sent my son to find out if the address and name are of a real person, and to deliver it. If this letter reaches you, (that is, if you are a real person) please read it, and if it means anything to you keep it. Otherwise you may just tear it up and throw it away; and forgive this intrusion." He had given his name and address. I opened the other large sheet. The handwriting on it seemed to be different. It began: "This is a message for Krishna from his wife Susila who recently passed over. . . . She has been seeking all these months some means of expressing herself to her husband, but the opportunity has occurred only today, when she found the present gentleman a very suitable medium of expression. Through him she is happy to communicate. She wants her husband to know that she is quite happy in another region, and wants him also to eradicate the grief in his mind. We are nearer each other than you understand. And I'm always watching him and the child. . . ."

It was very baffling. I stared at the boy. I made nothing

(119)

of it. "Boy, what is this?" "I don't know, sir. My father has been trying to send that for a week and could do it only to-day. I was searching everywhere; and I couldn't get away from my class, . . ."

"Oh, stop, stop all that, boy. Why has your father sent this letter to me?"

"I don't know, sir." I stood there and read it again and again and as my head cooled I was seized with elation.

"Take me to your house," I cried.

"It's far off, sir. In the village Tayur. . . ." It was on the other side of the river, a couple of miles off.

"No matter, I will come with you. What is your father?"

"He looks after his garden and lands in the village, sir. I read in the Board High School. I had leave to-day in the last period and so could bring you this letter."

"Good boy, good boy, take me to your father." I walked beside him. The child would be waiting at home. "One min-ute, will you come with me to my house? I will give you coffee and sweets. We will go. . . ."

"No, no, sir. I have to go away soon. I have to do some work at . . ." I tried to persuade him. But he was adamant. So was I. Finally we agreed upon a compromise. He gave me directions to reach his house. He'd go ahead and wait for me at the crossing and take me to his place. As I saw him go off towards the river, a sudden fear and doubt seized me. Suppose I should never meet him again. It was a horrible thought. "Boy," I had to beg him, "are you sure to wait?"

"Yes, yes. I will stand on the trunk road."

"If you will wait here a moment, I'll run home, get back and join you," I said. If it had been any work other than seeing the child. . . . The boy said: "I will wait for you at the trunk road positively, even if you are very late." "Good boy, good boy," I cried and raced home. The child was dressed and ready, waiting for me at the door.

As we left the kitchen and came to the hall, I told her: "To-day the little dear will go out with Granny—because father has to go out on business. . . ." She remained thoughtful and asked: "What business! Have you to go to college again?"

"No. I've to go and see someone, very important business."

"When will you come back?"

"As usual. But if you feel sleepy before I come, you just sleep. . . ."

"I won't do that," she replied. "I will go with Granny. She has promised to show me a small doll's house which has electric light. Won't you buy one for me?"

"Well, see it first, we will buy it later."

"Buy me a small house—this size," she showed me her thumbnail size, "with dolls so small."

"Where can you buy it?"

The old lady answered "It is not for sale; it is a small house kept in that medicine shop for decoration. . . ." I remembered seeing a small plywood doll's house kept in a small medicine seller's shop front. He sold some home-made pills; it was more or less a quack shop which gave medicine under no known system, but the shop was always crowded. In the centre of his shop he had mounted on a stand a plywood house with electric light. . . . It was hard to understand what purpose it served there. But perhaps its real purpose was to interest a person like Leela. . . .

I put on a shirt and an upper cloth and rushed out—along Ellamman Street, down river, crossing at Nallappa's Grove. As I passed it I could not help looking at the southern wall of the cremation ground far off. Smoke was climbing over its walls. Jingling bullock carts, talkative villagers returning home from the town, and a miscellaneous crowd on the dusty path leading to the Tayur Road on the other side. The sun inclined to the west. If I did not reach the crossroad before dusk I'd never be able to spot the boy. I almost ran up the road, and I reached the crossroad, where the boy had promised to wait for me. There I was. The west was ablaze with the sun below the horizon. Dusk would soon fall on us. But there was no sign of the boy. "Boy, Boy," I cried; not having asked him his name. Birds twittered on the trees, passers-by moved about, and my voice cried to the evening "Boy, Boy." What a fool I was not to have asked his name or precise directions!

"Boy, Boy," I shouted like a madman and passers-by looked at me curiously. I searched about frantically, and in the end saw the fellow coming up a path across the fields. "Sorry to be late, excuse me, sir."

"Good boy," I cried. "You are very kind to come." I liked him. I said to myself that I would do him all the kindness possible when he came my way again. He would get a lot of marks from me when he came to college. I asked him about his school, books, teachers and all sorts of other things as we walked on.

"That's our house." He pointed at the sloping tiles visible through the dense cluster of trees. A mongrel came and jumped at the boy: "Oh, keep quiet, Tiger. Go and tell father that a gentleman has come to see him." Tiger listened with his head tilted and at the mention of father bounced off in the direction of the house, vaulting over the gate of thorns and brambles. By the time we reached the gate, it was opened from the other side and a chubby and cheerful-looking person came towards me extending his hands. He had such good cheer in his face that it melted all the strangeness of the situation. He gripped my hand and said: "You must forgive the trouble I have given you. You must have thought it was a call from a lunatic asylum!" He laughed, "Oh, not at all, not at all," I muttered idiotically. I was too confused. My feelings were all in a mess. I didn't know whether I was happy or unhappy. I was excited and muddled.

He said: "You see, I would have searched you out, but it seemed too wild, and I thought it was all a fool's errand. I was most surprised to hear there was such a person. I hope you are the person. . . ."

"I'm the person, name, initials, and address and in regard

to the other things. . . . Have you known my name before. . . .?"

"Good God, no! You mustn't think so! I sent the letter as a test with the boy. I sent it out just as I got it, including the address. . . . I sent it out with the boy . . . and you could have blown me over with a breath, in spite of my size, when the boy came and told me that he had delivered the letter. I thought the boy was playing a practical joke, but he said you were coming. Are you sure you are yourself?" he asked with a rich quiet laugh. It'd be wrong to say that he laughed. . . . He hardly made any special sound or noise, but it was there all the time, a permanent background against which all his speech and gestures occurred, something like the melody of a veena string from which music arises and ends. "Come in, come in, we have a lot of things to say to each other," he said, and took me in through his small gate. The dog followed. He patted its back and said: "Nice animal, isn't it? I'm very fond of him. I don't much fancy the sentimental cynicism of some dog lovers who say that they prefer dog to man! It's nonsense. A dog is a nice fellow to have around. Though an animate creature, when you don't like him you can put him away, out of sight and hearing. He will obey you cheerfully. He never talks back."

I looked about. It looked like a green haven. Acres and acres of trees, shrubs and orchards. Far off, casuarina leaves murmured. "Beyond that casuarina, would you believe it I have a lotus pond, and on its bank a temple, the most lovely ruin that you ever saw! I was in ecstacy when I found that these delightful things were included in the lot."

"I'd love to see that temple, what temple is it?"

"The Goddess. It is said that *Sankara* when he passed this way built it at night, by merely chanting her name over the earth, and it stood up, because the villagers hereabouts asked for it. The Goddess is known as *Vak Matha*, the mother who came out of a syllable. Would you like to see it? But first rest and refreshment and then the other things of life. This has always been my motto. Shall we sit down here?" We sat down on a stone bench under a spreading mango tree. He pointed at the cottage and said: "You must also come in and see my home. I've a little library too. Here comes my wife." He introduced me to her as the unknown man for whom a letter was sent. She looked at me and said: "We wouldn't believe you really existed. I thought it was some joke of my husband's—won't you have some coffee and fruits?" She went in and brought a tray-load of good things. My host ate heartily, talking all the time; he told me numerous things about himself and the farm. How he purchased these acres eight years ago, and had worked on them night and day. He liked the pond, the temple and the trees, he wanted to be out of town, but near enough to be able to run into it. "My views have always been that it must be a quiet retreat, but a railway line must be visible from your veranda or at least a trunk road. Now we've both. If you sit here for a while longer, you will see the Madras mail passing over that ridge. I came here, so near the town, but you know for eight years I've hardly moved out of this estate. I'm quite happy where I am. By the way, my wife thinks if I moved up and down a little more into the town, I could occupy less space in my house. As if town-going were a sort of slimming exercise!" I listened to it all with only partial interest. I was very anxious to hear more about that letter and other matters connected with it.

"Shall we go around and see things?" He fetched two staves from a cluster strung on the fork of the mango tree, and gave one to me. He explained: "When an odd twig catches my eye I cut it off and make a stick. Tree twigs have a sense of humour and adopt funny shapes. I think it is one of Nature's expressions of humour. If only we can see them that way. . . ." He pointed at his collection: crooked, piked, stunted, awry, all shapes and kinds were there. "It is better to carry a staff, there are a lot of cobras about. Though I've never killed one in my life. When I see a snake I usually cry for help."

We wandered about the garden. He spoke incessantly, bursting with mirth, and explaining his garden. All the time he was talking my mind was elsewhere, in a hopeless tension, waiting to hear about the letter. I hoped he would open the subject himself. But he spoke on about all sorts of other things. I tried once or twice to ask him but checked myself and remained quiet. Somehow, I felt too shy to open the topic —like a newly-wed blushing at the mention of his wife.

It was nearly dark when we came to the northern edge of the estate. It was ineffably lovely—a small pond with blue lotus; a row of stone steps leading down to the water. Tall casuarina trees swayed and murmured over the banks. A crescent moon peeped behind the foliage. On the bank on our side stood a small shrine, its concrete walls green with age, and its little dome showing cracks; it had a small portal, and a flagstaff at the entrance.

There was a small platform on the threshold of the temple. The temple was locked. We washed our feet and sat on the platform; it appeared an enchanting place. We squatted on the platform. "Shall I have the temple opened?" he asked.

"No, don't worry about it now," I said.

"There is an old priest who occasionally comes here once a month or so. . . . A very fine man, with whom it is a pleasure to talk. A very learned man. I'm really afraid of him. He is too good for this place; but comes here only out of piety, and he is running some charity institution in the town. He treats this as an opportunity to worship the Goddess. . . ." He talked, I listened to him in silence. My mind was trembling with eagerness. I listened in tense silence. He asked with a smile: "You think I'm a bore?"

"Oh, no."

"Doubtless, you want to know all about that letter. . . ."

"Of course I'm very eager," I said, and added with a pathetic foolishness: "It was so long ago ..." I stopped abruptly not knowing how to finish the sentence.

"Now listen," he said: "Of late I have got into the habit of spending more and more of my evenings all alone here on this pyol. This casuarina and the setting sun and the river create a sort of peace to which I've become more and more addicted. I spend long hours here, and desire nothing better than to be left here to this peace. It gives one the feeling that it is a place which belongs to Eternity, and that it will not be touched by time or disease or decay. One day before starting for this place I felt a great urge to bring writing materials with me. Since the morning it had hung on my mind. I felt that an old sin of my undergraduate days of writing prose-poems was returning, but there was no harm in succumbing to it. I slipped a pad and a pencil into my pocket when I started out in the evening on my rounds. I sat down on this pyol with the pencil and pad. For some time I could write nothing; it seemed that a hundred ideas were clamouring to express themselves, crowding into my head. It was a lovely sky. I felt I must write something of this great beauty in my lines. Let me assure you that I'm by no means a poetical-minded fellow. I'm a dead sober farmer . . . but what was this thing within? I felt a queer change taking place within me.

"It was dusk when I sat down with the pad and pencil. Before the light should be fully gone I wanted to write down my verse or drama or whatever it was that was troubling me.

"I poised the pencil over the paper. Presently the pencil moved. . . . I was struck with the ease with which it moved. I was pleased. All the function my fingers had was to hold the pencil, nothing more. . . . 'Thank you' began the page. 'Here we are, a band of spirits who've been working to bridge the gulf between life and after-life. We have been looking about for a medium through whom we could communicate. There is hardly any personality on earth who does not obstruct our effort. But we're glad we've found you. . . . Please, help us, by literally lending us a hand—your hand, and we will do the rest.' I replied, 'I'm honoured, I will do whatever I can.'

" 'You need do nothing more than sit here one or two evenings of the week, relax your mind, and think of us.' 'The pleasure is mine,' I said. And then my hand wrote: 'Here is Susila, wife of Krishna, but as yet she is unable to communicate by herself. But by and by she will be an adept in it. Will you kindly send the following as coming from her to her husband.' And then I received the message I sent you and they also gave me your name and address!"

§

Our next meeting was a week later; on the following Wednesday. He brought with him a pad of paper, and a couple of pencils, and a pencil sharpener. "I don't want to risk a broken pencil," he remarked. "There must be no complaint of any omission on my part," he explained.

The casuarina looked more enchanting than ever. Purple lotus bloomed on the pond surface. Gentle ripples splashed against the bank. The murmur of the casuarina provided the music for the great occasion. We took our seats on the pyol of the little shrine. My friend shut his eyes and prayed: "Great souls, here we are. You have vouchsafed to us a vision for peace and understanding. Here we are ready to serve in the cause of illumination." He sat with his eyes shut, and as the dusk gathered around us, utter silence reigned. I too sat, not knowing what we waited for. The casuarina murmured and hushed, the ripples splashed on the shore. A bright star appeared in the sky. I almost held my breath as I waited. There was such a peace in the air that I felt that even if nothing happened this was a rich experience—a glimpse of eternal peace. We sat in silence, not speaking a word to each other. I felt we could spend the rest of our life sitting there thus. He poised his pencil over the pad and waited. Suddenly the pencil began to move. Letters appeared on the paper. The pencil quivered as if with life. It moved at a terrific speed across the paper; it looked as though my friend could not hold it in check. It scratched the paper and tore the lines up into shreds and came through. The scratching it made drowned all other sounds. It seemed to be possessed of tremendous power. My friend said with a smile: "I think my wrist will be dislocated at this rate, unless I have my wits about me. . . ." Sheet after sheet was covered thus with scribbling, hardly clear or legible—not a word of it could be deciphered. It looked like the work of a very young child with paper and pencil. By the light of a lantern he tried to make it out and burst into a laugh: "This writing does me no credit. If I leave it behind, it will be a headache for future epigraphists!" He looked at it again and again and laughed very happily. "I remember that for writing precisely this sort of thing, my teacher broke my knuckles once."

He put it away. After a few minutes interval he took his pencil to the paper again. His hand wrote: "We are here, trying to express ourselves. Sorry if you find our force too much for you. It is because you are not accustomed to this pressure. Please steady yourself and slow down. You will have better results. . . ."

"I have the feeling of a crow flying in a storm," my friend muttered to me. . . . But I . . . I suppose I must control myself. I am fat enough. . . ."

He gripped the pencil as in a vice and steadied himself. "No, no," his hand wrote, "You must relax, you must not set your teeth and get down to it so resolutely." His hand wrote: "Relax, slow down, control yourself, even if you feel like rushing off."

"Rather a difficult combination of things. This relaxed control; till this moment I never imagined such a combination existed," he muttered. He put away the pencil for a minute, stretched his arm, cracked his fingers and picked up the pencil again and turned over a clean sheet of paper. He said: "Great souls, I'm ready." Scrawled-up sheets of paper lay on one side. "This is better. Go on slowly. Check yourself

(128)

whenever you feel like running on fast. You will get good results." His hand steadied, his handwriting improved. The blank sheet was filling up. Letters and words danced their way into existence.

"We are sorry to put you to this trouble. But please understand that this work may revolutionize human ideas, and that you are playing a vital part in it. This is an attempt to turn the other side of the medal of existence, which is called Death. . . . Please go on for just half an hour to-day and then stop, or if there are unfinished messages, a maximum of forty minutes. And don't attempt it again for a week more, that is, exactly this same hour, next week this day. We have to warn you that it will take some more sittings before your friend here gets accurate results, but for a start what are you going to receive to-day will be quite good. Now put away your pencil and then start after five minutes. Your nerves are too much in a tremble, and they must subside. . . ." My friend put away the pencil, and said to me: "Are you happy? The next batch of messages may be from your wife." "I don't know how to thank you," I said. We watched the stars on their course for a few minutes; and gazed idly at the pond. Five minutes passed. He picked up his pencil and placed it over the paper. "Your condition is better. Remember our instructions. Stop in half an hour." "I will remember," he replied and asked aloud, "Is my friend's wife here?" "Yes. She is here," his hand wrote, and the words covered half a page. My friend exercised control over his fingers, checked and presently the writing assumed normal form. His hand wrote: "Your friend's wife has been here all along. In fact we are at this task mainly for her sake. She is so eager to communicate with her husband." I looked about. The semi-dark air seemed to glisten with radiant presences—like myriad dewdrops sparkling on the grass on a sunny morning. I strained my eyes and mind to catch a glimpse of these presences.

I told my friend: "Please ask if my wife will be able to communicate now directly. . . ." In answer his hand wrote:

"She is very much excited and she is also not able to collect her thoughts easily. At the moment, she finds it easier to tell us. . . ." I visualized her all a-tremble with excitement as on that day when I went to her place to see and approve the future bride. As I waited in the hall I caught a glimpse of her in another room through a looking-glass, agitated and trembling! I had never again seen her so excited. There fell a pause, as my friend's pencil waited. There did not seem to be any need to ask or answer. This was enough. The greatest abiding rapture which could always stay, and not recede or fall into an anti-climax like most mortal joys. After a few moments, I asked, "Do you remember the name of our child?" The pencil wrote: "Yes, Radha." This was disappointing. My child was Leela. I was seized with a hopeless feeling of disappointment. To be unable to recollect the name of the child! What was wrong? Where? My mind buzzed with questions. "The lady is smiling at the agitation which this name is causing her husband, but assures him that he need not feel so miserable over it. We've warned you that results will not be very accurate to-day. There are difficulties. We will do our best and gradually all these handicaps will be removed. Meanwhile understand that this is as good as it can be."

I asked: "But our child's name? Could this ever escape your mind?"

"No. It can't and it has not. You commit the mistake of thinking that she is responsible for giving that name. As a matter of fact it is a piece of your friend's own mind. You see there are particular difficulties in regard to proper names. We try to get through a particular name, for instance your daughter's . . . but since we use the mechanism of your friend's writing, more often than not his mind interferes, bringing up its own selections. This is how you got Radha now." "But how is this difficulty to be surmounted?" I asked. "Is there no hope at all?" I asked. "Yes, yes, by and by. Even now you may remember we could get through your name and address the other day and he was able to send for you. But it was an exception: he was ideally unselfconscious and his mind was very passive. It will all depend upon our friend's ability to remain passive, and keep his own thoughts out of the field. That's why we have asked him to stop in half an hour, which is the maximum time he can hold his ideas in the background." My friend said: "No. I can manage a little longer." "No. Half an hour will do. . . . But by and by you may go on even longer. . . . Please stop after this. The lady wants to say that she is as deeply devoted to her husband and child and the family as ever. She watches over them and prays for their welfare—only she is able to see things far more clearly than when she was on Earth, although you are not aware of my presence at times. . . . God's blessing be upon you and the child!" The pencil ceased. My friend looked at me as if to say: "Go on. Get up. It is over." But I was reluctant. So many questions to ask. My heart choked with the questions still unasked: "Just a second more," I pleaded. "I have just one more question." I paused. It was not clear to me what the question was. I pondered. "Can't we have it sooner than next week? . . . Please . . . Does she remember? . . ." It was no use. The pencil stood unmoving. We waited for a moment. And then my friend said: "They are gone. We will try again next week."

§

On the following week we sat there just at the same hour, with the dusk falling about us. They wrote: "We are here. Conditions are favourable. But remember our instructions and go slowly. Susila, wife of Krishna, is here and will now go on by herself."

"I have watched you since we met last and seen your mind. I saw the doubts crossing and recrossing your mind regarding identity. Naturally. How can you believe what you can't see? It might be me or someone else; was that not the line of thought going on in your mind? Correct me if I am wrong."

"You are right, absolutely right," I answered. It did not

(131)

require much self-scrutiny to see it. "And so I decided to clear this doubt first. And all this interval I have been trying to master the art of communication, and our helpers here have been very good to teach me. This is the first step. I hope you like this. I hope I do well for a start."

"Very well, very well, for a start. . . ." I replied in Tamil.

"I had not learnt very grammatical Tamil in my days, and if there are any mistakes, don't laugh at me."

"Oh, you are very good. You wrote beautiful letters," I said.

"And yet you have destroyed every one of them!" she said. "You found it possible to destroy every one of them!" she repeated. I was startled. No one knew about it. In the secrecy of night, on that day her condition was declared to be hopeless, I sat in my room, bolted the door, took out of my drawer several bundles of letters she had written to me, tore them up into minute bits and burnt them, and I also did the same with a few diary pages I had kept in the first years of our married life. I remembered saying to myself, gritting my teeth: "Let life do its worst, this is my answer. Every shred of memory will be destroyed, I will avoid torment thus. . . ."

"How have you come to know of it?" I asked.

"By watching your mind. I saw you yesterday as you pulled out your table drawer and reflected. I might not have known it at all if you hadn't reflected on it every day. For on the occasion you were performing the deed, I was, you remember, passing over, and in that transition stage one is not aware of things. It takes some time before we are able to know things. You have destroyed not only all that I wrote, but also all the letters you wrote to me. Was that the reason why you demanded them back from me every time I came back to you from my parents?" It was an unwritten law existing between us; whenever we were parted we wrote to each other on alternate days, and when we met again, I took back from her all the letters, bundled them up, and offered to destroy them, but she always protested and I just kept them with me.

(132)

"Why did you do it?" she persisted.

"I am very sorry. I thought I might abolish memory!"

"Have you been able to forget? Wasn't it childish to work your temper on those letters?"

"It seemed that memory would torment me."

"That's how it may appear at first sight; but later, let me tell you that you will have a desire to be surrounded by everything belonging to the departed. Just a turn of the wheel. A man takes to drink to forget sad thoughts, but after a while they return with gathered force. I understand your feelings but can only laugh at the remedy." I felt really like a child who had misbehaved. "Please forgive me if I appear to be speaking more than I ought. But I felt very unhappy about it. So this. I hope you will forgive this outburst," she said.

"You are perfectly right, and entitled to it," I said. "God bless you. I felt so vacant yesterday, when I had a longing to see your handwriting and could not find a single letter anywhere," I confessed.

"The lady is laughing," the Helpers said. "She is shaking with laughter. She says don't take anything too tragically—not even this!"

"I accept your advice. . . ." I said.

"You need not be unduly docile," she said, "and strain yourself to be agreeable, just because I'm speaking from this side. Don't hesitate to correct me if I appear silly."

"Oh, no, no, you are very sensible," I said.

"You used to be so considerate on the first two days whenever we met after a visit to my parents. You would not contradict anything I said. Here is a piece of news for you. There are about fourteen letters which have been spared. . . . I don't remember whether they were yours or mine, but I remember tying them up in a bundle; you will find them either in my trunk, or in one of the boxes in my father's place."

I thought over this and said: "I'm afraid you are wrong. There is not one letter left. I destroyed every bit that we wrote to each other."

"I'm sure of these fourteen: I remember the number precisely. I counted them, I tied them up and did not give them to you because you were very busy with something or other. I can't say how long ago; I put them away and then I remember coming across the bundle again and again. What I can't recollect is whether it was in my father's house or in ours. I am certain that the letters are there." She insisted: "Will you please make a thorough search once again?—and if you find them please don't repeat your previous act."

"No, no. I will be very careful," I said.

"Also, I want you to keep for my sake a sandalwood casket. I have put into it all my knick-knacks." I cast my mind about. I had looked through all her possessions and I had a knowledge of everything she had.

"I don't think you ever had such a box," I said. "Where is it?"

"It is not a very big box, about eight or ten inches long, three inches high and about four inches wide; the lid of the box is not flat but slightly elevated. I kept all my knick-knacks in it. It was given to me by my mother-in-law. Box of ivory and sandalwood. Please find it and keep it. I was fond of it. You may throw away all my other things. They are of no particular value to me."

"I can't throw out the tiniest speck that belonged to you. I will keep everything, including this box if I find it. But I'm not sure there is such a box."

At the next meeting she remarked: "You fret too much about the child. Have no kind of worry about her. When you are away at college, you hardly do your work with a free mind, all the time saying to yourself 'What is Leela doing? What is she doing?' Remember that she is perfectly happy all the afternoon, playing with that friend of hers in the next house, and listening to the stories of the old lady. Just about the time you return, she stands at the door and looks down the street for you. And when you see her you think that she has been there the whole day and feel miserable about it.

How you can help it, you never pause to consider. Do you know that she sometimes insists upon being taken to the little children's school, which is nearby? And the old lady, whenever she is free, takes her there and she has become quite a favourite there? Why don't you put her in that school? She will be quite happy there."

Immediately I contradicted: "I don't think she is going to a school. She would have told me about it. . . ."

"She went in casually once or twice, and perhaps forgot it later among other interests. I think she'll tell you when she remembers it. Anyway, if she likes it she may go there. . . ."

"All right, but is she not too young to be put to school?"

"She'll find it interesting, and it is not regular study. She can go and see other children and come home when she likes. . . ."

"I have no objection, but the teacher may have some other system."

"No. . . . It is a school meant for very small children."

"How much of the child do you see?" I asked.

"As much as anyone else, perhaps a little more. I have direct access to her heart now: I am always watching her."

"Does she see you?"

"Perhaps she does. Children are keener sighted by nature. She sees me, and perhaps takes it naturally, since children spontaneously see only the souls of persons. Children see spirit forms so often that it is natural to their condition and state of mind."

"If she sees you why doesn't she cry out?"

"It is a natural state to them, and in the depth of their soul they have certain reservations. Perhaps she doesn't speak out as much as she would like because she observes and understands the reserve you are all exercising in her presence about me. She merely saves your feelings by not speaking of me. You must have observed how little she refers to me. Did you think that it was out of forgetfulness? And don't you agree that there is a certain peace about her, which elders lack, although I was no less important to her than to anyone else?"

Nowadays I went about my work with a light heart. I felt as if a dead load had been lifted. The day seemed full of possibilities of surprise and joy. At home I devoted myself to my studies more energetically. The sense of futility was leaving me. I attended to my work earnestly. All the morning I sat preparing my day's lectures. My little daughter watched me curiously. "Father is reading!" she exclaimed. She drew a chair close to mine and sat up with a book, with any book that caught her fancy, till she saw a squirrel or a sparrow alighting on the roof of the opposite house, and exclaimed: "Father, the sparrow is come. Do they also read? Do they also go to school?"

"Little girl, just go out near the gate and ask," I said, with the idea of getting on with my work. Once she had gone out, she slowly got interested in something or other and forgot to come back. When she mentioned school, I pricked up my ears and was on the point of asking her a question, but I restrained myself, because I wanted to watch if the answer would come from her first or from the old lady. That very evening I heard the subject mentioned. When I returned home the child was out. There was only the old lady in the kitchen: I asked: "Where is Leela?"

"Oh, she has gone to the school," the old lady replied.

"Which school?" I asked with feigned ignorance.

"That baby's school, in the next street. I took her there once or twice in the afternoon, because she liked to see the other children, and they all like her very much there. To-day the teacher said he would bring her back in the evening. She wouldn't come away either: because she is making some animals and other things with clay. They have also given her scissors and coloured paper to cut. She is so happy!"

(136)

"Why didn't you tell me before that you had taken her there?"

"I took her out on two days just for a few minutes. When the child in the next house came home in the afternoon and went back to school, Leela also went with her one day," she said and added, "Poor thing, it was some way of engaging her mind and keeping her from longing for her mother!"

The child came home half an hour later. Her teacher left her at the gate and went away. "Father," she screamed at the gate, "I've been to school like you." I went out and picked her up in my arms. The teacher had moved off a few yards.

"Is that your teacher?" I asked.

"Yes."

"Call him," I said. At which she shouted: "Schoolmaster!" and the teacher turned back. "Come back and speak to my father."

"You are the headmaster of the school?" I asked.

"Yes."

"Is there any class to which this girl can be admitted?"

"Oh, yes. She will be happy. We shall be very glad to admit her." "Any long hours?" I asked.

"Oh, no, she can come any time and go away when she likes. No restrictions. Please send her. She will be happy with us."

"May I know your name?"

"Just Headmaster will do . . ." he said.

The child was dancing with joy. She was full of descriptions of her school. "Father, do you know I have made a clay *brinjal?* The teacher said it was nice." "All right, all right, I said, and sat by her side and made her take some tiffin which the old lady had prepared. She was too excited to relish anything. I coaxed her to eat. And then took her to the bathroom. Her face was streaked with the clay she had been handling. I soaked a towel in water and rubbed her cheeks till they glowed. And then I sent her in to the old lady and had her hair combed.

(137)

I took her out on her usual walk. I took her through the busy thoroughfare of Market Road. She loved the bustle of Market Road and kept asking questions and I found her view of life enchanting. I bought her some sweets at the stores. She mainly talked about her school. "Father, at our school, I have a friend. You know her father gives her lots of sweets every day. Why do you always give me only one or two?"

"Children must not eat more than two at a time," I replied.

"She is a good girl, always plays with me at school," the child said. "Shall I also grow tall when I go to school?"

"Yes, certainly."

"Why do you go to that far off school, and not to our school, father?" she said. She saw some villagers moving about with turbans on their heads. She asked: "Do they wear those things on their heads, even when they sleep?" I don't know what idea crossed her mind at such times. I took her to the river bank. She ran about on the sand. She watched the other children playing. She whispered: "That girl is in our school."

"What is her name?"

"Kamala," she said.

"Is she your friend?"

"She is a very good girl."

"Go and play with her if you like." The girl was playing with another group around a circle on the sand. At my suggestion Leela blinked and said with great seriousness: "She will be very angry if I ask to be taken also."

"Call her, let me see," I said.

"Kamala, Kamala," she called faintly, and then added: "That is her school name, she doesn't like to be called so when she is not in school." We passed on. She stood near other girls also and pointed them out to me as her school friends, but she would not go near anyone or call aloud. She seemed to identify her friends in a general way, whatever might be their names and their schools; as far as she was concerned they were all her friends and schoolmates. She was endowing each of them with any character she chose.

Next morning there was great activity. She was to be put to school. I was as excited as if I myself were to be put to school. I did little work at my table that day. I ran about the house in great excitement. I opened her trunk and picked out a shirt and skirt, fresh ones, printed cotton. When she saw them my daughter put them back and insisted upon wearing something in lace and silk. "Baby, you must not go to school wearing laced clothes. Have you ever seen me going with any lace on?"

"It's because you have no lace skirts, that is all," she said. "No, father, I want that for school. Otherwise they will not allow me in." She threw her clothes about and picked up a deep green, with a resplendent lace three inches wide, and a red skirt studded with stars: the whole thing was too gorgeous for a school. Her mother had selected them for her on a birthday, at the Bombay Cloth Emporium. Two evenings before the birthday we had gone there, and after an hour's search she picked up these bits for the child, who was delighted with the selection. I protested against it and was told, "Gaudy! There is nothing gaudy where children are concerned, particularly if they are girls. Whom are these for if they are not meant to be worn by children?"

"Go on, go on," I said cynically. "Buy yourself two of the same pattern if you are so fond of it." But the cynicism was lost on her. She disarmed me by taking it literally and said: "No, no. I don't think they weave sarees of this pattern? Do they?" she asked turning to the shopman.

The child was excessively fond of this piece and on every occasion attempted to wear it. To-day she was so adamant that I had to yield to her. She tried to wear them immediately, but I said: "After your hair is combed and you have bathed. . . ." And now as I put her clothes back in the box she grew very impatient and demanded: "Bathe me, father, bathe me, father." I turned her over to the old lady's care and arranged the box, carefully folded and kept away her clothes. She had over forty skirts and shirts. Her mother believed in stitching clothes for her whenever she had no other work to do, and all the child's grandparents and uncles and aunts constantly sent her silk pieces and clothes ever since the day she was born. The result was she had accumulated an unmanageable quantity of costly clothes, and it was one of my important occupations in life to keep count of them.

She was ready, dressed in a regalia, and stood before me, a miniature version of her mother. "Let us go," she said, and for a moment I was unaware whether the mother or the daughter was speaking—the turn of the head and lips!

"I must carry books," she insisted.

"No, no, not to-day. . . ."

"My teacher will be angry if I don't take my books," she said, and picked up her usual catalogue. She clasped it to her little bosom, and walked out with me, bubbling with anticipation and joy.

The school was in the next street. A small compound and a few trees and a small brick-red building. The noise those children made reached me as I turned the street. The schoolmaster received us at the gate. As soon as we entered the gate, a few other children surrounded Leela and took her away. She left me without a thought. She behaved as if she had been in that school for years and years.

The headmaster was in raptures over the new arrival. He said: "Won't you come and have a look round?"

He had partitioned the main hall into a number of rooms. The partition screens could all be seen, filled with glittering alphabets and pictures drawn by children—a look at it seemed to explain the created universe. You could find everything you wanted—men, trees, and animals, skies and rivers. "All these—work of our children . . ." he explained proudly. "Wonderful creatures! It is wonderful how much they can see and do! I tell you, sir, live in their midst and you will want nothing else in life." He took me round. In that narrow space he had crammed every conceivable plaything for children, see-saws, swings, sand heaps and ladders. "These are the classrooms," he said. "Not for them. For us elders to learn. Just watch them for a while." They were digging into the sand, running up the ladder, swinging, sliding down slopes—all so happy. "This is the meaning of the word joy —in its purest sense. We can learn a great deal watching them and playing with them. When we are qualified we can enter their life . . ." he said. The place was dotted with the coloured dresses of these children, bundles of joy and play. "When I watch them, I get a glimpse of some purpose in existence and creation." He struck me as an extraordinary man.

"If they are always playing when do they study?"

"Just as they play—I gather them together and talk to them and take them in and show them writing on boards. They learn more that way. Everybody speaks of the gameway in studies but nobody really practises it. It becomes more the subject of a paper in some pompous conference and brings a title or preferment to the educational administrator. Oh, don't allow me to speak too much on this subject as you will find me a terrible bore. . . ." He was a slight man, who looked scraggy; evidently he didn't care for himself sufficiently. His hair fell on his nape, not because he wanted it to grow that way, but, I was sure, because he neglected to get it cut. His coat was frayed and unpressed. I liked him immensely. I was sure there were many things about him which would fascinate me. I was seized with a desire to know more of him. I asked him: "Please visit me some day."

"I will certainly drop in one day when I take a holiday. You see I hate holidays. It is ten or fifteen years since I began this work, and I have not felt the need for a holiday at all. Holidays bore me. And I spend even my Sundays here looking about. This is a nice place; there is a garden too, entirely made by children." He took me through a bamboo stile to a small plot with tiny lots. He was continually enthusiastic. "Does he ever sleep?" I asked myself. "Come to my house on a Sunday instead of coming here," I said and he agreed. I had a feeling that I was about to make a profound contact in life.

§

The next sitting was a complete disappointment to me. But perhaps my own frame of mind was somewhat to blame. After the first thrill of discovery subsided, I fell into a questioning mood and asked, the moment my friend was ready with the pencil: "Do you remember the last day we went out together?"

"Yes, I remember."

"Can you say where we went and a few incidents of the day and so on?" I asked.

"I remember going out on the last day with you. I feel we visited a temple, bought something for the child, and also visited a painted house. We went out followed by the servant and did a little marketing on the way."

"Oh!" I said. "What else do you remember?" The pencil paused for a while and then scratched off: "We met a scorpion on the way and you nearly put your foot on it. We bought a brass lamp used for worship, and a toy engine."

"Do you remember what happened in the house we visited?" I asked.

"No," she replied.

"Absolutely nothing happened?" I asked. In answer to it the Helper wrote: "The low roof of the kitchen knocked her head, and she is laughing because her husband slipped in the backyard. . . ."

"To be frank this did not happen. I don't know why she is saying these things," I said.

"She promises to do better next time," the Helpers wrote. "There are some difficulties both in expressing and picking out of memory the exact items. We would advise you to stop now. The lady sends her love and prayers for her husband and child. . . ." And they were gone. The hand stopped. "Half an hour over I suppose," said my friend. I rose to go home very unhappily. Except one or two references, the rest was all too wild. . . . I grumbled and went home in a most unhappy state of mind. "To be in this state till next Wednesday."

But a week passed. I was back there on the following Wednesday. Meanwhile I had scrutinized the pages again and again, and came to the conclusion that after all they were not so wild. Each detail was correct, temple, painted house, buying for the child and the lamps. Every time she went to her parents she purchased brass lamps and knick-knacks for someone or other; a toy engine was bought on the last day for the child. As for knocking her head against the kitchen roof, she was rather tall for her age and was very proud of the fact that most doorways were too short for her and that they knocked her on the head, and she always spoke about it. I could not recollect when I had slipped in the backyard, but otherwise each individual item seemed to be after all correct, though chronologically mixed up in utter confusion. I mentioned it to my friend when I met him next and his explanation seemed to be plausible: "I will ask you a question now at short notice. When did you buy the cloth for this shirt?" I looked at my blue shirt helplessly. "Was it before or after you purchased the coat you are wearing over it? And on your way home from the shop that day what else did you buy and how much? You see how difficult it is to place these exactly, while you are still living in the midst of these experiences. I can't say for instance what exactly I had for dinner this day last week. . . . While chronological order and precision in details are so difficult for us, they must be more so to other beings whose surroundings are timeless and entirely different. If my speculation is right their vision of things embrace an experience as a whole rather than events in an order. All memories merge and telescope when the time element between them is removed. I think this is the reason for the apparent confusion. Add to this the possibility of their memory being finer and more selective; there may be a natural law operating by which unpleasant memories and impressions are filtered and left behind with the physical body. If you take all this into consideration, you may view their inaccuracies more charitably."

§

At every sitting she urged me on to look for her sandal-wood casket and the fourteen letters. I couldn't search very thoroughly because I found it impossible to enter her room and open her trunks. On a holiday afternoon I steeled myself to it. I opened the door and felt a pang at heart when I cast a look around at her trunks, her clothes and possessions. "For all of us our possessions turn to mementoes. Is there any one in the whole world who can say his lot is different?" I reflected, as I sat down amidst her trunks. My daughter was thrilled to see me there, and cancelled an appointment she had with her friend and joined me in my search.

I opened Susila's yellow trunk, in which she kept all kinds of toilet sets she had acquired in her lifetime. Three or four different coloured vulcanite cases with mirrors and small bottles. She used to be very fond of these boxes and asked for one whenever she saw them in the shop—green, orange, red, of all colours. I took them out one by one. And then all kinds of cardboard boxes and fancy tin containers stuffed with embroidery thread and woollen bits. The small sweater in yellow—she had been reading about knitting and had become suddenly very enthusiastic. She behaved like a child in her enthusiasm. Every day as I left for college she gave me a commission for a purchase on my way back. It was rarely I was able to pick up the correct colour that she wanted, and I had the task of exchanging it for the correct shade next evening. Finally, exasperated, I arbitrarily forced her

to begin work on the yellow sweater for me. She sat down on
the veranda step and plied her needles by the evening light,
refusing to go out on a walk or do anything else. Night and
day she thought and spoke of nothing else. At the end of
the day the two shining needles were stuck into the ball and
kept on a shelf in the hall. I made all kinds of jokes about
it, saying that the sweater seemed to be promised for my
hundredth birthday and so on. The back of the sweater was
nearly ready and she looked triumphant. The ball of wool
was satisfactorily going down in bulk. She proclaimed that
the complete sweater would be on my back in eight days; and
then our child caught a cold, and she lost all peace of mind
and could not knit; thereafter one thing and another inter-
vened and she never took it up again at all. In that condition it was still lying in the box, with the yellow back ready,
the needles stuck, as they were on that day, into the ball of
wool. "What is this, father?" the child asked picking it up.
I shook my head and said: "Put it away, girl, you may hurt
yourself with the needles." And then there were fancy borders meant to be stitched into some dress. I had always protested against the purchase of these things and she always
waived my protest away with: "You just see how they look
when they are stitched into my jackets and the baby's
frocks! You will yourself ransack all the shops for more of
them." But they were still where they had been put the day
she bought them. This box contained a couple of fancy lacquer caskets of Burmese origin, which her sister from Ran-
goon had sent; they were filled with small bottles of scent,
which I had given her during the first two years of our married life. I opened their corks one by one and smelt them.
Their delicate perfume brought immediately around me other
days. Evenings when we went out, and spoke of nothing in
particular, first years of married life when I used to be very
vehement about my plans for the future. These tiny phials
had compressed in them the essence of her personality, the
rustle of her dress, her footfalls, laughter, her voice, and

the light in her eyes, the perfume of her presence. The bottles were empty now but the lingering scent in them covered for a brief moment the gulf between the present and the past. I shut my eyes and dwelt in that ecstasy: I reflected: "Of all the senses it is smell which is the subtlest; it takes you back to the core of your experience. Why have they not studied its laws and processes, while they have studied all the other senses? Do these scents mean anything to her in her present state?"

"What are you smelling, father?" asked the child and brought me back to the earth. "Why are you closing your eyes, father?"

I drew down the lid. There was no trace of the fourteen letters and the sandalwood casket. I opened another trunk in which she had kept her clothes—dozens of sarees and a hundred and one jackets of all colours and shades; and above all else that glittering gold-woven purple saree, in which she was presented to me as a bride on the all-important day. Many of these clothes had not been taken out more than once because she had a dread of spoiling their sheen.

She picked up like a child every soap-box carton and empty container and preserved them in her cupboard and put into them coins and knick-knacks. In a cardboard box I found stuffed a few sheets of paper. I pulled them out. They were embroidery designs copied in pencil, and some recipe for a tooth powder. There was a sheet on which she had even begun a story with childlike simplicity of two brothers, woodcutters, one of whom was good and industrious and the other was lazy and bad. There were my corrections in between the lines. I remembered how on a certain day she sat for hours at my table stroking her lips with the pencil, lost in thought. I do not know what made her want to write a story at all. . . . But she was filled with shame when I found her out, and was so nervous when I read through it and corrected the grammar; she never proceeded beyond the first page of the story, where the brothers differ and separate. . . .

This seemed to me a precious document now crumpled and stuffed into the box. I carefully smoothed it out, and took it with me to my own table.

The child sat very quietly watching me and derived a great deal of pleasure in arranging the empty tins side by side. . . . There was still powder in one of the tins, three quarters full, bought a month before she fell ill. I opened the lid and smelt it. "You are once again shutting your eyes," remarked my daughter.

§

At the next meeting, the moment my friend was ready with the pencil, she asked: "Do you know what a wonderful perfume I have put on! I wish you could smell it. . . . On second thoughts I had better not mention it because you will want to smell it and feel disappointed. Perhaps it may look like selfishness for me to be so happy here when there you are so sorrowfilled and unhappy. . . . It would hardly be right if I produced that impressoin. If I succeed in making you feel that I am quite happy over here and that you must not be sorry for me, I will be satisfied. Your sorrow hurts us. I hope our joy and happiness will please and soothe you. . . ."

"Undoubtedly," I replied. "But what makes you mention the perfume?" I asked.

"Just to enable you to have the most complete idea of our state of existence, that is all. Moreover, did you not speculate somewhat on those lines a few days ago?"

"How do you spend your time usually?" I asked.

"Time in your sense does not exist for us," she replied. "Our life is one of thought and experience. Thought is something which has solidity and power, and as in all existence ours is also a life of aspiration, striving, and joy. A considerable portion of our state is taken up in meditation, and our greatest ecstasy is in feeling the Divine Light flooding us. . . . We've ample leisure. We are not constrained to spend it in any particular manner. We have no need for exercise as we have no physical bodies. Music is ever with us here, and it transports us to higher planes. . . . Things here are far more intense than on earth; that means our efforts are far more efficient than yours. If by good fortune we are able to establish a contact with our dear ones who are receptive to our influence, then you say that that person is inspired. And a song or melody can establish a link between our minds, for instance, how sad that you should have neglected your veena. If you could take it up once again our minds could more easily join. Why don't you try it?"

It was years since I had put it away. I had a gift for it when I was young. "I don't know scientific music. I have been after all a self-taught amateur. . . ."

"Do not worry what anyone will think of your veena. For me it will be the most welcome music. I promise that you will feel my presence as you have never felt it yet. It will surely make your heart easier.

"You might have thought I did not very much care for music when on earth, but as a matter of fact I was really intensely interested in it . . ." she said. I remembered how quietly she liked music. She never took great pains to learn it although she could sing well. She could never be persuaded to sing; but sometimes unaware of my watching, she would sing to herself while combing her hair or putting the child to sleep. If I showed any signs of listening she would stop. She always listened to music wherever it came from—a gramophone in a house on the way, or a beggar singing; she listened with a silent rapture.

"You think I have become a very learned sort of person and all that kind of stuff?"

"Yes," I replied. Ever since these communications began I felt, now and then, that she showed a greater wisdom than I had known her to possess. "You would much rather that I was the same prattling person I was on earth, but let me tell you that the change that takes place when one comes over here is so great and the vision is so cleared that even I, your

(148)

wife, whose nonsense pleased you so much more, am changed. I'm essentially the same person as far as you and my dear ones are concerned, but the only difference is that I'm without the encumbrance of the physical body and everything is finer and quicker than on earth.

"Between thought and fulfilment there is no interval. Thought is fulfilment, motion and everything. That is the main difference between our physical state and yours. In your state a thought to be realized must always be followed by effort directed towards conquering obstructions and inertia —that is the nature of the material world. But in our condition no such obstruction exists. When I think of you or you of me I am at your side. Music directly transports us. When I think of a garment, it is on me. In our world there is such a fine response for thought. When I come to you I prepare myself every time as befits the occasion. I come to meet my lord and I dress myself as befits the occasion. I think of the subtlest perfume and it already pervades my being; and I think of the garment that will most please you: the wedding saree, shimmering purple woven with gold, I have on me at this very moment. You think you saw it in that trunk, how can it be here? What you have seen is its counterpart, the real part of the thing is that which is in thought, and it can never be lost or destroyed or put away."

Thereafter she mentioned at the close of every evening her appearance. "Have no shadow of doubt that I'm here. I am wearing a pale orange dress with a clasp of brilliants to hold it in position."

"What a gorgeous dress!" I exclaimed.

"If only you saw the colour you would not say how gorgeous, you would be speechless. Not even the colours of sunset give you such tints as we have here; to call it pale orange is to give you an idea as inadequate as the idea which a child forms when . . ."

I cast a look around. She at once said: "You look round. I can see you. What a pity you can't see me! Some day let us hope you will see my form. I am at the moment sitting to your left on the floor with my arm resting on your lap, and directing your friend's hand by my thought." I looked down at my lap. "No use yet, even if you open your eyes so wide. But by and by, you will hear my bangles clanking and feast your eyes on my dress and form.

"I think I look the same person as on earth. Only free from all ailments, ills, and cares. You remember I used to have a sort of pain at the waist, even that I do not have now.

"My dress tonight is a shimmering blue interwoven with light and stars. I have done my hair parted on the left. (And what a load of jasmine and other rare flowers I've in my hair for your sake!) I wish a painter could sense me and do a picture for you. . . .

"Rest assured that I shall always sit in the same place whenever I am here; when you lift your arm you touch me. At the close of this evening when you go home, I will accompany you, stay up with you till you go to bed and fall asleep thinking of me. . . .

"If you want any evidence of my presence, pluck about ten jasmine buds and keep them near your pillow to-night. Before I go away I will take their scent with me: that I can do. You will see the difference when you smell the flowers in the morning."

On my way home, through the dark night, across Nallappa's Grove my feet felt lighter, because I knew she was accompanying me. Her presence was unmistakably there. I could sense it. The darkness of the night was not felt by me. The distance and loneliness were nothing to me. She was with me. I quietly enjoyed the fact without stirring the slightest thought. Far off I saw the dark night lit with the fire of a cremation. But it did not disturb me! "I know more than this . . ." I remarked.

CHAPTER SIX

SUNDAY. I decided to spend the entire day in the company of the child. Of late my college work and the extra activities and the weekly visits to my friend took up so much of my time that I spent less than two hours a day with the child. It was a painful realization. "Oh, God," went up my prayer, "save me from becoming too absorbed in anything to look after the child properly." And I felt very sorry and guilty when I returned home at nights and found the child asleep.

She had her own plans for the day. As soon as she got up and was ready for the road, she insisted upon being taken to the school. "This is Sunday, you don't have to go," I pleaded.

But it was no use. "You don't know about our school. We have school." She put on her coat and stepped out. I went out with her. "Why do you follow me, father?" she asked.

"I too want to see your school to-day," I said.

"But my friends are filled with fear if they see you. Don't come with me, father," she pleaded.

"No, I will take good care not to frighten them," I assured her. She stood for a moment undecided, looking at me and said to herself: "Poor father, let him come too," and smiled patronizingly.

There was no sign at the school to show that it was a Sunday. It was alive with the shouts of children—about twenty of them had already gathered and were running about and playing: the swings and see-saw were all in full use. The headmaster was with them.

"You don't rest even on a Sunday?" I asked the head-master.

"Rest? This is all right for a rest, what else should I do? They just come in, play, throw the sand about, and go away, and we also do it with them. It is quite good, you know. I feel quite happy. What else should I do on a Sunday?"

"Something to differentiate it from other days. . . ."

"Quite. We don't do sums to-day. We just sing, hear stories, and play. . . ." His eyes were red. He coughed. He did not look as if he had had sleep at night.

"What is the matter with you?" I could not help asking.

"I suffer from sleeplessness, my friend," he said. "It is some years since I had anything like sleep. I sleep about an hour. I used to make myself very miserable about it at first. But now I am used to it. I make up stories for children and I hardly feel the time passing. Come in and see." He took me into his room. It was thatch-roofed. Its floor was covered with clay, and the walls were of bamboo splinters filled in with mud. The floor was uneven and cool, and the whole place smelt of Mother Earth. It was a pleasing smell, and seemed to take us back to some primeval simplicity, intimately bound up with earth and mud and dust. Along the wall was a sort of running ledge covered with a crazy variety of objects: cardboard houses, paper flowers, clumsy drawings and bead work. "These are the work of children who have studied here, and some of them have a special significance: presented to me by the outgoing children or the very special effort of a child. They are the trophies of this school. I consider them a real source of joy. For instance, the very first work of a child has some peculiar value. I don't know if others understand that there is anything in it at all . . . you will understand it better if I say look at that green paper boat. Can you guess who has made it? Your daughter on the very first day she came here, she finished it within an hour." I felt thrilled. Beside a parrot cut out of a cardboard picture and an inkpot made of paper, this green boat stood.

I went over and picked it up. My little Leela in relation to an outside world, making her own mark on it: I was filled with pride and satisfaction. "It is a whaler with a knife-edge at the keel!" I cried in joy. He jumped out of his seat: "That's what I say. See how lovely it is!" The sight of it filled him with a mystic ecstasy. "She is a grand child. So are the other children. The first work of almost every child is here and the other works go into the general hall." The walls were hung with different pictures, tigers and lions and trees drawn with childish hands. He swept his hands about and declared: "Every one of these is children's work. They are the real gods on earth." He stopped before each picture and enjoyed the thrill of it anew. He had done away with table and chair. In a corner he had a seat for visitors. "This will do for a school. We are a poor country, and we can do without luxuries. Why do we want anything more than a shed and a few mats and open air? This is not a cold country for all the heavy furniture and elaborate buildings. This has cost me just fifty rupees, and I had three such built. But we have not much use for them, most of our time being spent outside, under the tree. . . ."

"Many people think," I said, "that you can't have a school unless you have invested a few thousands in building and furniture."

"It is all mere copying," he replied. "Multiply your expenses, and look to the Government for support, and sell your soul to the Government for the grant. This is the history of our educational movement. And another thing. What a fuss they have learnt to make of sports! As if colleges and schools were gymnasia, the main business of which is to turn out sturdy idiots. When I think of all the pampering and sentimentality of sports and games!" He shuddered. "The main business of an educational institution is to shape the mind and character and of course games have their value. Why worship sports, and the eleven stalwart idiots who bring in a shield or a cup? It is all a curse, copying, copy-

(153)

ing, copying. We could as well have been born monkeys to justify our powers of imitation."

"Yes," I said. "In our college Brown forgoes even his club to see a match; loses himself in excitement, congratulates the team and shakes hands, and gives no end of liberties to the tournament players and even sends them on tour," I said, catching the infection of his mood.

"And do you know, they not only get a lot more touring and tiffin than the others. They are even made to pass examinations! And this sort of thing is supposed to make our people modern and vigorous. . . ." He laughed, but the excitement was too much for him, and he subsided into a fit of coughing.

"I'm sorry," he said. "Sit down, sit down. I wanted to show you the stories I've made. . . ." He pulled out a box and brought out a big bundle of brown paper: huge pages covered with letters as well as figures cut out and pasted. "This is a new method which I find fascinating," he said. "I invent a story, write it down in words, and illustrate it with pictures cut out of illustrated books and papers and pasted at the appropriate places, for instance this," he threw down ten volumes, "is a pretty long story of a bison and a tiger in the forest . . . just glance through it." Every page had a figure or two; the illustrations ran along with the story.

"They are almost real you know," he said as I gazed on the pictures. "Just watch, I'll show you how it works." He stood in the doorway and announced: "Story! Story!" The children who had been playing about, stopped, looked at him and came running in, uttering shrieks of joy.

They sat around their master. When they subsided into silence he opened the large album and said looking at it: "This is the story of a tiger and his friend the jungle buffalo, called Bison. It happened in Mempi Forest. Who can tell me where Mempi Forest is?" There followed a discussion among the children and one girl said pointing at the doorway: "There, near those mountains, am I right?"

"Right, right," he said. "There are a lot of jungles there. See here." All the children leaned over each other's shoulders and fixed their eyes on the top of the album where a perfect jungle had been made with the help of dry tinted grass pasted together. "These are all bamboo jungles, full of tigers, but we are only concerned with one tiger. His name is Raja. See this. There he is, a young cub."

"He is very young," said the children, looking at him. The album was passed round for the benefit of those sitting far off. "What a fearful fellow!" commented a few. My daughter, sitting between two friends older than herself, refused to touch the album because of the tiger, but was quite prepared to see it if held by her neighbour. "This little tiger was quite lonely, you know, because her mother had been taken away by hunters—bad fellows." Thus the story of the tiger went on. The tiger came across a friend in the shape of a young bison, who protected him from a bear and other enemies. They both lived in a cave at the tail end of Mempi Hills— great friends. The bison grew up into a thick rock-like animal, and the tiger also grew up and went out in search of prey at nights. One night a party of hunters shot at the bison and carried him off to the town. And the tiger missed his friend and his cry rang through the Mempi Forest the whole night. The tiger soon adjusted himself to a lonely existence.

The children listened in dead silence and were greatly moved when this portion was read out. They all came over to have a look at the tiger in his loneliness, and our friend, rightly guessing that they would ask for it, had procured a picture. The tiger was standing forlorn before his cave. The children uttered many cries of regret and unhappiness. "Master, how can he live without his friend any more? I hope he is not killed by the bear!"

"No. No, that bear was disposed of by the friend before he was caught."

"Poor bear! Let me have a look at him," said a girl. The

pages were turned back and there he was, dark and shaggy. "He could have fought with the bison. He looks so strong," said the girl. She was, somehow, unaccountably, on the side of the bear. "You should not like the bear," said another girl. "The teacher will be angry if you like the bear. . . ."

"No, no, I won't be. You may like what you like," said the teacher. This was an inducement for another child to join the ranks of bear-lovers. She said: "I always like a bear. It has such a lot of hair. Who will comb her hair, teacher?" "Of course, her mother," said another child.

"Has she a mother? Poor thing, yet she was allowed to be killed by the bison. I don't like bisons. They should have more hair!"

"If you are so fond of bears, why do you listen to this story?"

"Because it's the story of a bear, of course," replied the child.

"It isn't."

"It is. You see the picture."

"Master, she is looking too long at the bear. I want to see the tiger." The teacher interfered at this stage and restored order. He whispered to me: "The most enchanting thing among children is their quarrels. How they carry it on for its own sake, without the slightest bitterness or any memory of it later. This is how we were once, God help us: this too is what we have turned out to be!" He resumed the story. My daughter, who felt she had left me alone too long, came over and sat with her elbows resting on my lap. She whispered: "Father, I want a tiger."

"A real one?"

"Yes. Isn't it like a cat?" I nudged the teacher, and told him of her demand. He became very serious and said: "You must not think of a tiger as a pet, darling. It is a very big and bad animal. I will show you a tiger when a circus comes to the town next. Meanwhile you may have a picture of a tiger. I will give you one."

(156)

"All right, master, I will take it."

"And you can have a real cat. I will give you a small kitten I have at home."

She screamed with joy. "Is it in your house?"

"Yes, yes. I will give it to you and also the picture of a tiger."

"Father, let us go with him. . . . ."

"Surely surely," the teacher looked delighted. "Come with me. . . ." He went on for a few minutes more and ceased. The story would run on for a full week. He stopped because the clock struck twelve. The children wouldn't get up. The tiger had just been caught by a circus man for training. The children wanted to know more and more. "Master, you mustn't stop. What happens to the tiger? Is he happy?" He would answer none of their questions. He ruthlessly shut his books and got up.

"We are hungry, teacher. We will go home."

"That's why I stopped the story. Go home and come and listen to it to-morrow," he said.

"Do they kill the tiger?" asked the child.

"No, no, he is quite safe. He will be quite all right, trust me," said the teacher. The children, greatly pleased, ran out of the school. My daughter asked: "Is it the same circus you promised to take me to?"

"Ah, something like it. Here too you will see a tiger," he replied and we got up. He locked the shed and the gate and walked down with us. When we reached our house, my daughter insisted upon going with him though she was hungry. He cajoled and coaxed her to go in. But she was adamant. At which he offered to come in and wait for the girl to finish her food and then take her with him. I seated him in my study.

"This is the book I read," the girl said placing the big catalogue in his hand. He turned over its leaves and was lost in its pictures. I took her in to dine. I told the old lady: "There is another person for dinner to-day. Can you manage?"

"Oh, yes," she said, although I knew she'd give her share of food or cook again. I invited the headmaster to sit down with me. He looked happy and at the same time uncomfortable: "My wife at home, she will be waiting. . . ."

"Won't she guess you won't be in?" I asked. "Come on." He yielded.

It was a most delightful party. I found him more and more fascinating. He took off his coat, folded up his sleeves, and asked: "Where is the bathroom? I should like to have a wash." He came out of the bathroom and said: (his face wet with water and hands dripping) "Don't offer me a towel please. . . ."

"Then how do you dry it?"

"I just leave it alone, and it will evaporate. I never use a towel."

"Why, fear of infection?"

"I don't know. I have never liked a towel, not even my own. Even after a bath I just keep standing till the water evaporates, and then put on my dress with the result that every day my wife creates a most fearful row outside the bathroom, because you know it takes a little time for a wholesale drying like that."

My daughter was delighted that her teacher was dining with us. She was sitting down in her place with her silver plate in front of her, and was half-way through her rice. But when she saw her teacher she exclaimed with joy: "I will also eat with teacher," and tried to get up. She was, however, pressed back into her seat. She was very unhappy. "Eat slowly, but don't get up. Eat slowly till your teacher joins us," I said. The teacher would want some more time for himself. "Please grant me fifteen minutes. I usually pray and meditate for fifteen minutes before dinner, the only time that I can spare. Just fifteen minutes. . . . Another thing that seems to upset my wife." His wife seemed to be weighing on his mind. He muttered: "I could have managed well as a bachelor, but they wouldn't let me alone." There was something very appealing in the way he spoke. He spoke of himself as if it were someone else. His own life seemed to give him as much amusement as he found the company of children inspiring. I found a place for him to sit and meditate, left him alone and came away. He preferred the back courtyard facing the east. He squatted on the floor and closed his eyes and was lost in it. He was completely wrapped in his own vision for quite a long while, and then came and joined me. He did not seem to have the slightest feeling of being in a stranger's house. He conducted himself as if he were in his own house. As he came into the dining room and took his seat on the plank next to mine he asked: "What have you done for dinner? I hope I have not put you to great difficulty or extra trouble?"

"Oh, no. Some simple fare. I hope you won't find it too bad. . . ." The usual courtesies were going on in the usual manner, and he said suddenly: "Don't you think we have evolved some silly social customs? For instance . . ." Now as the old lady served us on the leaf the first course, fried brinjals, "I am not very fond of this. But can I say so?" He gently pushed it away to a corner of the leaf: "Please forgive me if I don't touch it. I would sooner swallow poison than eat brinjal. . . ." A most eccentric man. But we had almost arrived at a tacit understanding to be strictly truthful rather than formal. So I replied: "Well, I won't apologize for it, you know. If you don't like it, it is a pity. I hope you will like something else presently. . . ."

"That's right. I like to speak and hear only on these lines. This is the simplicity to which all human conduct must be reduced. This is what the company of children has taught me. A fact which makes it very difficult for me to manage in an adult society. But then why should I ever try to get on with adults?" My daughter remarked: "Our master doesn't look like himself without his coat." He usually wore a loose, colourless coat, buttoned up to his neck. Now without it he certainly looked different. He looked rather young and slight.

He seemed to put away ten years when he took off his coat. Indistinct features, greying at the temples, pouches under the red eyes. With all this there was a touch of freshness about him. My daughter asked: "Tell me a story, teacher. . . ."

"No, no, we must never tell stories while eating. Only at school. What should we do at school, if we had spent all the stories at home while eating?"

After food he reclined on the mat in the hall. My daughter placed before him a plate of betel leaves and arecanut. He chewed them with contentment. His lips became as red as his eyes. He looked very happy. The child sat nestling close to him and exhibited to him all her toys; the scores of coloured utensils, and brass miniature vessels, the rubber balls and her big doll. She carried the doll on her arm and said: "This girl wants to come with me every day to school. She cries and shouts every day. What shall I do, master?"

He looked at the doll and said: "Not a bad girl." He pretended to pinch its cheeks and said: "See how soft she is. . . ." My daughter was greatly pleased. She looked at the doll affectionately and said: "She is a most lovely girl, master. But she does want to go with me to school, what shall I do?"

"Do you want to bring her or not?" She shook her head sadly. "No, master. She is a bad baby and will give a lot of trouble at the school. She will not allow me to study there. She will quarrel with everyone." Certain inescapable antisocial characteristics of this doll seemed to sadden Leela, but she had steeled herself to a sort of resignation. So her teacher said: "Well, why don't you lock her up in a box when you come to school?" Leela shook her head: "That I can't do because she will die. I will lock her up in a room."

The teacher asked: "Do you mind if I lie down and rest a while?" He lay down and shut his eyes. My daughter insisted upon lying down beside him. Soon she was fast asleep. So was he. I went away to my room, picked up a book, lay on my camp easy chair, and dozed.

We were all ready to start out at four in the afternoon, my daughter persistently asking for a cat.

§

We walked down the road. His house was in Anderson Lane, which was a furlong east of my house—a locality we had never visited. It was a street within a street, and a lane tucked away into a lane. There was every sign that the municipality had forgotten the existence of this part of the town. Yet it seemed to maintain a certain degree of sanitation, mainly with the help of the sun, wind, and rain. The sun burned so severely most months that bacteria and infection turned to ashes. The place had a general clean up when the high winds rose before the monsoon set in, and whirled into a column the paper scraps, garbage, egg-shells, and leaves; the column precipitated itself into the adjoining street, and thence to the next and so on, till, perhaps, it reached a main thoroughfare where the municipal sanitary staff worked, if they worked anywhere at all. And it was followed by a good wash down, when the rains descended in November and December and flushed the streets, and water flowed along the roadway and joined the river.

Malgudi had earned notoriety for its municipal affairs. The management was in the hands of a council with a president, a vice-president, and ten elected members; they met on the last Saturday of every month and battled against each other. One constantly read of disputed elections, walk-outs, and no-confidence motions. Otherwise they seemed to do little by way of municipal work. However, when a distinguished visitor came to the town, the president and the members led him up the stairs of a tower in the municipal building and from there pointed out to him with great pride Sarayu cutting across the northern boundary of the town, glistening like a scimitar in moonlight.

Carpenters, tinsmiths, egg-sellers and a miscellaneous lot of artisans and traders seemed gathered in this place. The street was littered with all kinds of things—wood shavings, egg shells, tin pieces and drying leaves. Dust was ankle deep. I wondered why my friend had selected this of all places. I was afraid to allow my daughter to walk here. I felt she would catch all kinds of dreadful diseases. Unkempt and wild-looking children rolled about in the dust, mangy dogs growled at us, donkeys stood at attention here and there. I offered to carry my daughter on my arm but she refused to be lifted. Her teacher said: "Don't worry, leave her alone. This is really a healthy place for all its appearance. She will be all right, don't worry about her too much. . . . No harm will come to her. . . ." I left her alone, rather abashed and feeling rather that I had been found out.

"Who is the Anderson of this lane?" I asked, looking at the impressive name-plate nailed on to the wall of a house.

"God knows. At least to honour the name I hope they do something for this place. . . . I have often tried to find out who Anderson was. But nobody seems to know. Perhaps some gentleman of the East India Company's days!"

He suddenly stopped and said: "Now this is my house." The tiles of the roof jutted into the street, a gutter gurgled and ran down in front of the house.

"Come on carefully, don't fall off into the gutter," he said.

As soon as we had crossed the gutter, three children of ages between seven and ten stood in the doorway and hugged him. "Is your mother at home?" he asked.

"No," they replied.

"Excellent," he said and went in. He looked relieved to hear it. "Now, young fellows, here is a new friend, see what a fine girl she is." The children looked at Leela with interest. Somehow this attention seemed to puzzle her. She gripped my hands tight and tried to get behind me. The children adjusted their positions so that she might still be within range. Finally she could stand it no longer. "Let us go, father. Where is the cat?"

"Wait, wait," I whispered. "You must not ask for it at

once. See how nice those children are." They weren't. They looked too wild. Their hair full of mud almost matted, their dress torn and dirty, an abnormal liveliness about them. They stood relentlessly staring at my child. Their father had slipped in and now came out with a roll of mat. He spread it in the passage, between the front door and the central hall, a large part of which was an open courtyard with a well in the middle; the whole place was unspeakably wet. The hall was choked with old furniture, clothes and vessels. Beyond was a narrow kitchen, black with soot. The mat was an old, tattered, Japanese one with a girl holding a parasol painted in the centre. I and my child sat down. The three children stood around gazing. He asked: "Where is your mother gone?"

"We don't know. We couldn't ask because she was angry you hadn't come. Why didn't you come home, father?" "I had somewhere else to go to," he replied lightly and tried to dismiss it from their minds. But they insisted until he said: "You mustn't keep asking the same question."

The eldest asked: "Have you had your food?"

"Yes."

They looked at each other and said: "Mother went away thinking that you wouldn't have eaten, and that you would come and ask for it."

"Not I," he said. "I know your mother—well, children you may all go away now . . . or take this baby with you and play with her." There was consternation in my daughter's face and she muttered: "Father, don't let them call me." He saw this and said: "You don't want to go with them? Then don't. Now you may all leave us." With a great shout they ran towards the street and vanished. I couldn't help asking: "Where are they going?"

"I don't know. I can't say—perhaps to the gutter, or to some low-class den in the neighbourhood. I've no control over them. They are their mother's special care, you know." There was a hint of a terrible domestic condition. I did not wish to pursue it. But I blundered into it. "Don't they attend your school?"

"They!" he repeated: "I could sooner get the Emperor's children. My school is for all the children in the world except my own."

"Where do they study?"

"You may know better. . . ." At this point a fat woman of about thirty-five, with sparse hair tied into a knot at the back of her head, her face shining with oil and perspiration, strode up the steps of the house. She threw a look at him and did not seem in the least to notice me sitting in the passage, though striding past us. She walked into the house, muttering: "So you have found the way home after all!" gritting her teeth. He didn't reply but merely looked at me sadly. She stood in the doorway of the house and said: "How long must I keep dinner waiting? Do you think I'm made of stone?"

"Nobody asked you to wait."

"You are not to decide who should wait and who should not. You and your school! You don't know the way back from your school, I suppose."

"Don't speak rubbish. Here is a cultured visitor, who will laugh at us."

"Let him, what do I care? If he is big, he is a big man to you. He is not a big man to me. What do I care? Answer me first. Where were you all the time? Do you think I'm a paid watchkeeper for this house?"

I could not watch this scene any longer. I got up and said: "We will be going." He looked at his wife and said: "I can't bring a gentleman to visit me without your driving him away with your fine behaviour."

"Oh, no, it is not . . ." I began.

She replied: "Ah, what a fine sermon. I'm not going to be another woman than myself even if the king is here. What did I do to him?"

"Don't take it . . ." I began, starting up. My daughter said: "The cat. He hasn't given me the cat." He said: "Right. I never meant to forget." He looked at his wife and asked: "Where is that kitten? Is it inside?"

"I don't know," the wife said. "I have too much to do to be keeping count of the cats and dogs that pass this way." He smiled at me weakly and said: "Can't get a straight answer from her, at any time of the day! There are people in this world who have rough tongues but who are soft at heart—but this lady! I look ridiculous, speaking of my wife in this manner. But why should I not? Children have taught me to speak plainly, without the varnish of the adult world. I don't care if it strikes anyone as odd." My daughter punctuated his narration with "Where is the cat?" I had the feeling that I ought to run away. So I said: "Perhaps it has gone out, he will bring it when it comes back home." He said, "Wait," and went in and looked about and returned shaking his head. "It used to be in the store behind that tin. Forgive me, baby. I will positively get you a cat soon." My daughter looked very disappointed. So I cheered her up with a joke or two and walked out. He followed us back to our house. He seemed to feel more at home in my house than in his. He reclined in the easy chair, pulled out a book and was soon lost in study. I looked at him in surprise. The book was a criticism of the Elizabethan dramatists, Beaumont and Fletcher. "This is the dullest work I've read in the English language. How is it that it interests you so much?"

He lowered the book, removed his silver spectacles and said, "I'm not reading it. If I open a book like this and allow my eyes to rest on the lines, it helps me to do a lot of private thinking. I read very few books for any other purpose. This book for instance, has helped me to reflect deeply and earnestly on the question of family, marriage, and such other institutions." My daughter came in and showed him a house she had made out of a matchbox. He seemed to forget all his troubles in an instant. "Oh, what a house, what a house. The only house worth having in this world," he added turning to me, as she went out, carrying it away with her. Her friends were at the gate calling for her, and she shouted, "Father, I'm going to play," and ran away and joined them. "She seems to have had enough of adults' company since this morning," he remarked, putting away Beaumont and Fletcher. He looked at the book and said with a smile "Not a line in the whole book to distract your thought —an ideal book for a contemplative turn of mind. . . . Not a line in it. . . ." He put away the book, remained silent for a moment and said: "Did you notice how quickly that child dropped us and joined her fellows? Adult company is unfit for angels. Adults who can't even keep a promise in regard to a kitten. Helpless fools we must appear to her. What wishy-washiness!"

It was nearing six. I looked over the wall of our next house, and saw my child playing with half a dozen children. I asked: "Come on, child, are you coming out with us for a walk." She hesitated. Her friend suggested: "Let us play here. Let father go out and return." She accepted the advice and said: "I am not coming, father, you may go."

I and the headmaster walked down to the river bank, sat on the sand, and watched the sunset. He told me: "Some twenty years ago when I passed my B.A. at the university, they wanted me to take law; and then wanted to rush me into an office chair, but I resisted. I loved children and wanted to start the school. How can anyone prevent me from doing what I want? I had been hustled into a marriage which did not interest me, and I was not going to be hustled into a profession I did not care for.

"I was the only son of my father, but he said such bitter things that I left home. We had a fine house in Lawley Extension, you wouldn't believe it. I was brought up there, it is the memory of those days which is rankling in my wife's heart and has made her so bad and mad. I walked out over the question of employment; and went back home only on the day he died. And then my wife thought I would occupy that house after his death, but not I. I don't know what he has done with it. He had married a second time after my mother died and I think she and her children or his brothers must be fighting for it. I don't want that house, I have no use for it, I don't want any of his money either. But my wife expects me to be fighting for these rights. I can't enjoy these rights even if I get them, and I think it is waste of one's precious hours of living to be engaged in a contest."

"But your wife and children could be in better circumstances. . . ."

"You think so? No chance of it, my friend. She will create just those surroundings for herself even in a palace."

"But you have not put her in a very happy locality. . . ."

"Perhaps not. But I chose it deliberately. It is where God resides. It is where we should live. And if we have any worth in us the place will change through our presence. But my wife does not believe in anything like it. She thinks my school a fool's idea; won't send the children there. I did my best. But it is no use. She has a right to send them where she likes. I think she sends them to the gutter and pig-sty; you saw what they are like. She is an impossible type. But my only hope is that there may be a miraculous transformation some day and that she may change. We should not despair for even the worst on earth."

"Till then don't you think you should concede to her wishes and move to a better place?"

"No. First because it is a duty for me, and secondly because she will carry the same surroundings wherever she goes. You see, the trouble is not external."

The river flowed on against the night. I listened to him; he appeared to me a man who had strayed into a wrong world.

"How did you get this idea of a school for children?" I asked.

"The memory of my own young days. Most of us forget

(167)

that grand period. But with me it has always been there. A time at which the colours of things are different, their depths greater, their magnitude greater, a most balanced and joyous condition of life; there was a natural state of joy over nothing in particular. And then our own schooling which put blinkers on to us; which persistently ruined this vision of things and made us into adults. It has always seemed to me that our teachers helped us to take a wrong turn. And I have always felt that for the future of mankind we should retain the original vision, and I'm trying a system of children's education. Just leave them alone and they will be all right. The Leave Alone System, which will make them wholesome human beings, and also help us, those who work along with them, to work off the curse of adulthood." He was seized with a fit of coughing. He recovered from it, paused, and said: "I will tell you a secret now. I strictly want to live according to my own plan of living and not subordinate it for anybody's sake, because the time at my disposal is very short. I know exactly when I am going to die. An astrologer, who has noted down every minute detail of my life, has fixed that for me. I know the exact hour when I shall be . . . that lady will have the surprise of her life," he said and chuckled. "That's why I'm so patient with her."

We walked back home. I invited him in: "No, no, not fair. But be assured I shall make myself completely at home whenever I like. I hope you won't mind."

"Not at all," I replied. "Treat this as your own home."

"Good Lord! No. Let it always be your home," he said with a smile and bade me good night.

CHAPTER SEVEN

I MISSED my friend's sittings continuously for three or four weeks. He was ill for a few days, and then he had some work or other on hand, and then guests, all of which prevented his giving me a sitting. I went there and turned back with a feeling of disappointment, and on the fourth Wednesday I went there hoping again. There was only a garden servant to answer me. My friend had left a note behind: "Awfully sorry. Have had to start for Trichinopoly on some urgent business, at an hour's notice. Can't say when I shall be returning, but I will write to you." He had gone with his entire family. I asked: "May I go and rest a while near the pond?" The servant gave me permission. I sat there on the pyol of the shrine as the evening declined. The still surface of the pond, the lotus, the evening breeze, all had a reviving effect, but the sense of disappointment was very keen within me. I shut my eyes and visualized the form of my wife. The casuarina murmured. I said aloud: "Are you all here, can't you devise some means of communicating with me, o great spirits?" I felt ridiculous talking to myself thus. My words fell on a deep silence and died without a response—the faintest would have made me happy, but it was not there. I repeated my appeal in a low tone and felt ashamed of myself for appearing to be talking to myself. For the first time in months, I felt desolate. The awful irresponsiveness of Death overwhelmed me again. It unnerved me. All the old moods returned now. It looked as though they had been in bondage all these days and were now suddenly unleashed. I was overwhelmed.

I went home and slept badly that night. I kept asking myself: "I have been clinging to the veriest straw, thinking that I was on land. Now the straw has snapped and I know my position. I can only drown. I'm drowned, and did not know it all these days. I was clinging to a grass blade at the brink of a well." I went about my business next day with a heavy heart. As soon as she saw me in the morning my daughter was seized with a doubt and asked: "Father, you are angry!" "No, no," I said, and with a great effort of will played with her and saw her off to school. I hated my food, I hated my work, I loathed my friends. That day I continuously lost my temper with the boys. A student in the B.A. class rose in his seat to have a doubt cleared. He was a first-class student, always serious and well-behaved, but I snapped: "Will you sit down? I can't stand all these inter-ruptions. . . ."

"But, sir . . ."

"That'll do. Because you obtain more marks than your neighbours, you needn't . . ." He looked crushed, and sat down. I could never forget the expression on his face, nor forgive myself for it. At the end of the period I called him aside and said: "Well, what did you want?"

He at once mentioned his difficulty. I cleared it and added: "Don't worry so much about these things—they are trash, we are obliged to go through and pretend that we like them, but all the time the problem of living and dying is crushing us. . . ." "Yes, sir, but for the examination . . ." he added. And I said: "I'm sorry my dear fellow, if I have been rude to you. A lot of things are weighing on my mind. . . ." "I understand, sir," he said and went away. I showed less tol-erance to Gajapathy. At the quadrangle when we passed each other at the end of a day he said: "Krishnan, I must have a word with you." I stopped without a word and waited for him to speak. He said: "Can I speak to you now?" I said sharply: "Yes, why not now?" "Here?" he asked. "Yes, what's wrong with here?" "You seem to be upset over something." "Nothing. All is perfect in the world. I'm all attention." He took me to his room, seated me in a chair and said: "First, I want to tell you that Brown feels we have been neglecting the history of literature. He saw the test papers of the fourth year and is disappointed. He thinks the boys will ruin themselves in the public exam."

"Well, what are we to do?"

"He wants you to take a special period for them in the history of literature."

"Why do they make so much of the history of literature? They have to make a history of every damned thing on earth—as if literature could not survive without some fool compiling a bogus history. If he won't mind my saying this to the boys, I will accept the special classes. . . ."

"Don't be frivolous," Gajapathy said. "Your college habits have not left you yet. . . ."

"Far from it. I see more clearly now between fatuities and serious work."

He had grown more tolerant with me these days. He waited for me to finish my lecture and gave me his own advice and orders. "All right," I said. "I cannot but obey you. But I will tell the boys what's sense and what is nonsense. I will tell them that they are being fed on literary garbage and that we are all the paid servants of the garbage department."

§

As I was standing at the door of my house, Leela's teacher passed along the street. I saw him at a distance and tried to pretend I had not seen him and turned in. It vexed me to see people and talk to them. It was a tremendous strain. I sat in my room waiting for him to pass. But he stopped and cried "Krishnan." I was bound to meet him. I went to the gate and greeted him. I didn't like to call him in. So I rushed out to dispose of him in the doorway. He asked: "Not well?"

"Quite well. I have never been in better health."

"Coming out for a walk in the evening?"

"Sorry, I have another engagement."

"Where is your daughter?"

"Gone out to play." We carried on thus for a few minutes, for my part brief sentences and monosyllables.

Till late in the evening I sat alone at a corner of the river. "A long dip in this river, or a finger poked into a snake hole—there are two thousand ways of ending this misery. But the child, the child. . . . She will be looked after by God, and by everyone. She is an entity. She was able to go on without her mother, and she could equally well carry on without her father. I have put by a little money for her. . . . Well, she will be looked after quite well—God bless her." Far off I saw the glow of a funeral pyre over the walls of the cremation ground, and I sighed for it. It seemed to be the greatest aspiration one could have. "Exactly where she was placed and burnt. . . ." I recollected her pale face, with the flies on it, and the smile on her lips, and broke down at the memory. I recovered and said to myself: "This is also my end. Oh, God, send me to those flames at once." I saw a picture of myself being carried there and the funeral ceremonies. And this vision seemed to give me a little peace.

Thus days followed, bleak, dreary, and unhappy days, with a load on the mind. I felt as though I had been filled with molten lead.

And then came a letter one morning from my friend, "I'm sorry to have remained silent so long. I have been up to my ears in litigation and it looks as though all these affairs are going to take more and more of my time. But anyway, I will arrange these things and return in a few weeks. My house here is in the extension with a fine small compound, and a room all to myself, where I spend the larger part of my day in reading when I don't talk over matters with lawyers and witnesses. You see, I had to come away suddenly because an uncle of mine passed away, and there are all kinds of arrangements to be made in regard to property. He married three times and has numerous children, and you know how many complications can arise out of that!

"Anyway, my purpose in writing to you to-day is not to trouble you with my affairs, but a different one. I have a feeling that we might attempt an experiment while we are out of each other's reach. I want to see if we can manage a sitting—a sort of *in absentia* business. For spirit matters, space is of no account, and so there is no reason why we should not succeed. On Sunday at 4 o'clock in the evening I propose to try the experiment. So please keep yourself in your room and link up with me mentally with a request to your wife to communicate. As far as possible keep all other business from your mind. At precisely 4.30, you may consider it closed. I will send you the result of this sitting by post immediately."

This offered me a new lease of life. Two days before me. All the weariness melted.

On Sunday I cajoled my daughter into spending her time at the school with the old lady and then shut myself in my room and lay down in my chair and closed my eyes. The clock showed two minutes to four. I stilled myself. My heart was palpitating with excitement. I had to hold my breath for a moment before it could be stilled. I opened my eyes and saw that it was four and said: "Oh, dear wife, my friend at the other end and I have linked up. Please communicate." I visualized my friend sitting in his room, and I fancied myself occupying a chair beside him, and my wife communicating through him. I shut my eyes and remained in a sort of half-sleep till 4.35.

Two days later the postman brought me a long envelope, as I was just starting for the college. With the books under my arm, I tore open the letter, and pulled out two long sheets of paper covered over with pencil writing. There was a covering letter from my friend:

The message read: "It is a long time since I spoke to you through your friend. I have a feeling as if I were sitting on

(173)

a wall. On one side I see your big friend. On the other I see you, lying in your green canvas easy chair and also trying to be present here at the same time. . . . Seeing you now in your old chair, as you shut your eyes and try to keep your mind still, I forget for a moment that we are in two totally different mediums of existence. . . .

"The most important thing I wish to warn you about is not to allow your mind to be disturbed by anything. For some days now you have allowed your mind to become gloomy and unsettled. You are not keeping very strong either. You must keep yourself in better frame. . . .

"We must thank your friend who has yielded to our suggestion, to try these absent sittings. I'm sure you will benefit by them. Please think yourself as being able to establish communication with us direct. You will have to prepare yourself for it. There will be a change in your state. Moreover you should not expect your friend to be troubled by you all your life. You must make yourself fit for it, and this communication will restore to you health and better nerves because of the greater harmony that comes into your life; but you must also do your bit to utilize this harmony. You must keep your body and mind in perfect condition, before you aspire to become sensitive and receptive; I have learnt a great deal after coming here; believe me if it is peace of mind you want, you cannot have it better than from us. . . ."

"How do I become sensitive?" I asked.

The following Sunday we again linked up at the same hour. On Monday morning the postman brought me the message: "Don't feel sorry. It hurts me more than you can imagine. So please keep your mind free from choking thoughts. I wish to give you a picture in words.

"A weary and thirsty traveller was returning home from a long day's march. The setting sun had touched all the objects around him with a rosy magic. The birds were returning to their nests. A rumbling brook rolled along. He sat down and quenched his thirst with water. He saw a black

(174)

bird sit on a thorn and whistle. A batch of white cranes flew across, tinted by the sunset. Their rhythm and their colour filled the traveller's heart with an indescribable joy. He said to himself, 'Worshipping and wondering, how much life's journey is made easier for one who can see nature and God every moment!' He returned home fatigued in body, but his soul was in the rapture of a song.

"I don't know what you are going to make of this. Somehow, this picture has been haunting my soul all along: and a great inexplicable satisfaction reigns in my heart because I have communicated it to you. I have set a song to sing this to me. When I sit down and sing it, a most heavenly sunset, birds of wonderful colours, and the serenity of the brook, everything comes up palpably and we can even converse with the traveller. And the melody. It is just created out of thought, in a manner which you cannot grasp. The responses of our world are immediate and fine; you have a glimpse of it only in your striving; there your deeper mind impels you, there it is a striving; here it is an achievement. Your striving itself is proof of its reality here; to be realized when the obstructions of your state are cleared. . . .

"I don't know if you think I'm becoming a poet as well. I have given you many thoughts lately for writing by impressing them on your mind; you might have caught them if you had continued your old habit of occasionally writing verse. Some day I hope we shall together produce a great epic. I'm not joking. I'm in earnest. Nobody may think much of these efforts. They may appear, just as the picture of the weary traveller does, obvious or obscure to others, but certainly you will like them because they are your dear wife's efforts."

In about ten days my friend returned to his garden and we were able to have a sitting as before. I was very happy to be back at the old seat beside the lotus pond.

After the preliminary remarks and suggestions my wife asked abruptly: "When are you starting an attempt at your own psychic development?"

"How can I say?" I replied.

"Oh! if you do not know what you are going to do or not do, who else can?"

I felt snubbed and explained: "I didn't mean that. I should like to be told when and what to do. I look to you for guidance!"

"Why not make a start to-morrow? To-morrow is a day that never comes. Why not begin to-day as soon as you go home? Just ten minutes will be sufficient. Keep your mind free for impressions just for ten minutes. Just ten minutes of communion and relaxation. Please make the attempt and do not postpone it. You think of me by fits and starts. Sometimes for long periods you do not let your mind do anything else. I can only tell you that I am very happy here. I shall be very happy to meet you when you come over here don't doubt me, but it is not right for you to think of passing over before the appointed time. So do not let your thoughts go in that direction. It is to prevent it that I want you regularly to bring me to your side at a stated time."

"So you want me to think of you only at stated hours?"

"Yes, for the purpose of your complete communion with me or with anyone a degree of concentration is necessary and this can be done only with some order and plan. At other moments when you are despondent, woe-begone and hopelessly in grief and think of me, I can hardly come to you, because the grief creates a barrier, and this should be avoided for both our sakes."

"But look here," I pleaded. "How can I help having you as the permanent background to my thoughts? I can't help thinking of you. . . ."

"Just as I am thinking of you, I know you will also be thinking of me. But I want this thought to be coupled with the desire to commune with me. It is this aspect that I want to impress upon you as necessary for psychic development and free communion between us."

(176)

"So do you wish me to check thoughts of you at all other times?"

"No, no, no. At stated hours sit for psychic development, that is, to enable me to get into touch with you directly without the intervention of the medium; this I will make possible."

"Should I sit down with pencil and paper?"

"It is a secondary matter, pencil, paper and the rest. The most important thing is to get the mind ready and receptive, the actual form will follow automatically. Prepare your mind for this adventure. You will then know and feel my real presence. You now keep looking round to get a glimpse of me; then by and by, you will feel that I'm by your side, and it will bring real peace to your heart. Relax, be passive and think of me, and be receptive. Just ten minutes. Try."

"To-night?"

"Yes, to-night."

"It may be eleven before I'm ready."

"The time is immaterial."

I went home singing. I felt I had picked up the key to a new world. I had never known such joy before. I felt that my duty was now to conserve all the force of my mind for this communion.

At home, the child lay awake in bed. I went in to dine, and she came over and sat on my lap as I ate. I went to bed, stroked her forehead and she soon fell asleep. I put out the light, sat down and prayed: "I am ready."

I looked at the clock—ten to eleven. "My wife," I called. I had made it all too easy in my imagination. I thought I had only to say "be passive" to make the mind passive, "still" to be stilled, and I would see her standing radiantly— foolish expectation. I had to struggle with my mind. I desperately cried for her. My mind seethed with ideas—irrelevant things came rushing in, college, work, evening friends, my wife's voice—in the midst of it all I struggled to keep the mind receptive. It was a desperate fight. It nearly reduced me to tears. I tried to improve matters by picking up a pencil and poising it over the paper. Beyond the scratch that I inadvertently made, there was no result. I looked at the clock. Eleven-thirty nearly. I felt exhausted. I lay down to sleep, and slept badly.

§

The little peace and joy I had seemed to grasp suddenly once again receded, and I became hopelessly miserable. It was as if a person lost in an abyss found a ladder, and the ladder crumbled. When I went to my friend next Wednesday, I was all anxiety for further guidance. I hoped somehow that there was a magic password which would be imparted to me, whereby I would be able to walk hand in hand with my wife. But as soon as we were ready for it, she said: "At the last sitting I gave you advice about psychic development. Since then, I have been observing the struggle going on within you and your utter helplessness. To receive impressions from our side, the mind must be calm and unruffled. In your case, I find that thoughts of me produce just the opposite effect. I feel that it is too early and that the wound is still very raw. I think therefore you ought to postpone your attempts for some time, until you are less agitated than you are now. As it is, it does not serve the purpose I thought it would. So please do not bother now. Am I clear?" This made me more desperate. Even the ladder that I saw was removed and I was forbidden to go near it. I could almost hear her voice as she said this, slightly quivering with excitement, and with a touch of reprimand. I was in despair for a moment—but only for a moment. I became indignant. She couldn't deny me my right to attempt. I said: "I won't stop this attempt on any account. I feel quite confident I can go on." This had the desired effect, and she replied, "Oh, if you are feeling confident, it is another matter. But as I watch you, I find that your mind is very unprepared. This makes communication more difficult. So I suggest that you wait for some more time. Possibly there may be a change in your outlook. Then you will derive greater benefit. I'm not saying stop it at all costs. If you feel confident, go ahead. I am only indicating the circumstances that stand in the way." I felt very happy. And a regret seized me, as it always did, that I had perhaps been too sharp in my expression. So I felt I ought to be more considerate, and asked: "Oh, I'm glad, so may I continue my efforts, and will you do your best still?"

"Yes, continue then. If I can give you any further assistance, I will."

I asked testingly: "Just to know that you are aware of my efforts, can you tell me what you saw me do on these nights?"

"I am aware and I am present, but I cannot make myself known better because of the difficulty. I have seen you every night wanting contact with me and praying for it. You had a few sheets of paper and a green-handled pencil. . . ."

I had over a dozen pencils in my drawer; I hadn't noticed which one I had picked up that day.

She continued: "You put pencil to paper and hardly made a dot. . . . And this after trying without paper and pencil, at first. I am keen on impressing on you the fact that it will be possible for you to appreciate my presence even more than my physical presence in course of time, if the development takes place properly, that is, the necessary mental atmosphere is made available for me."

"Can you give me some details of where you saw me sit for communion?" I asked.

"I saw you sitting on your bed. You sat up with your eyes closed. You had just begun to concentrate when a carriage passed along the street, wheels rattling and the driver singing lustily—and you gnashed your teeth and said something very rough about him."

"I am so happy you feel the attempts I made at communication."

"I tell you I can feel your thoughts even when you are not exactly sitting for development. Even when you just think of me anywhere and everywhere, on the road, at home, or on the river-bank when a streak of moonlight lights the water surface, and you think of me, I feel it and know your thoughts. But development is necessary for the reverse process to take place, that is, for you to feel my thoughts."

This restored my peace of mind. "Calm, calm," I repeated to myself like a *mantra*. I blamed myself for not being aware of so simple a remedy. I think I sang lightly as I returned home that night. "Be calm, my dear fellow," I said.

Suddenly there dawned on me the meaning of her statement: "When you see the moonlight lighting up the water surface." Weeks ago, in my period of desolation, as I sat on the sands of Sarayu, a late moon rose in the east, and the flowing water shimmered with it. It only added to my desolation. Again, it reminded me of my wife. How often had she expressed a wish to walk along the river in moonlight, and for all the years of married life I had not been able to give her that fulfilment even once; some pointless thing postponed it every time; we never went out in moonlight at all. And this regret tormented me when I saw moonlight on water, that night. . . .

§

At our next meeting she said: "I still feel you have not done well. Why can't you postpone your attempt for a while?" I had been dreading this suggestion all along. Now it had come. I was not going to accept it. I said stubbornly: "No, I feel I can still try. I find these very attempts very beneficial. I want to continue them. Will you help me as much as you can?"

"I'm very happy to hear it. Why don't you change the time from night to morning and see if it will improve matters? Not more than ten minutes. I think after a night's sleep, such sleep as you can get, the attempts in the morning will be more successful."

"Early morning?" I asked apprehensively.

"No. After you get up and have your coffee, shut yourself in a room for ten minutes. At night your mind is not very receptive. All the day's affairs are there boiling up again and again. Sleep lulls your thoughts, and it may be you will succeed if you try then." I shook my head. She said: "Just try for ten days." I was somehow very reluctant to try in daylight—there was all the hurry for school and college, the attention to the child, the shutting the door on her (she was sure to bang on it), the visitors or tradesmen who might call on me, and above all the daylight. The softness of night was essentially psychic, I felt. So I said: "I don't usually feel very fresh in the mornings. I still think night is the best. . . ."

"Well, get on with your attempts at night then," she said. I was seized with a sudden fear. Suppose she said this out of despair, unable to coax me out of my obstinacy. So I asked with trepidation: "Will you be present whatever the time?"

"I shall be present morning, noon or night. Don't worry. Just go on as usual, but with greater relaxation and ease. No harm in trying with paper and pencil too; when you feel an urge, please relax and let your hand move. If you keep a pencil, it helps concentration."

"How will you make me feel your presence?"

"At first it will be a matter of belief—a belief in the possibility of my presence. Later on as you progress, you will know I'm there by your side. I have high hopes of making myself heard or seen, but certainly known; I shall be with you very soon."

"I shall continue my attempts whatever happens," I said gratefully.

"I'm trying to make matters easier and more rapid for your development. I know you sense my presence, but I feared that you might give up all attempts at communication if you did not get messages from me sufficiently early. I feared that you might then feel that your awareness of my presence was imaginary and give up the attempt for ever. That's why I wanted you to postpone rather than run the risk of losing faith. . . ."

I was greatly moved at hearing this: "It is enough that I feel you are there. Don't trouble yourself to give me any sort of proof. It is not necessary."

§

For a fortnight I tried to follow her instructions rigidly. I relaxed with a vengeance. I kept my mind open. I posted a sentry at the threshold of my mind to stop and turn away any intruder who might try to gain entrance. I rigorously educated by whole being, including the subconscious, (where still perhaps lurked unsuspected raw grief) with the suggestion that my wife was everywhere, happy and well, and I was to think of her only with the greatest joy in mind; no cause for any sort of grief. I lay down on my bed, and then pictured her as I had known her in her best days, and centred my mind on this image without the slightest wavering for ten minutes. I felt very satisfied with my effort till on a subsequent evening she said: "I must tell you now that your sittings for development must be even more relaxed than they are at present. Why don't you allow your mind to move round about me? Now you just picture me in your mind and do not allow your thoughts to move an inch this side or that. This rigid exercise does not help our contact. By your intense and severe thought you make almost a stone image of me in your brain. Your thoughts must give me greater scope for movement within an orbit of feelings. Your mind may now be compared to the body of a yogi who sits motionless. This is not what you seek to achieve, do you? I want you to keep your mind at these times open for my impression. What happens now is that your mind is full of your thoughts of me, which are unrelaxed, and I find it difficult to move about in your head and heart.

"The only trouble now is that your mind is rigid. Till lately I'd even greater difficulty because of your poignant sorrow. This barrier is now lifted more or less. What is still required is that you should be able to receive my thoughts. It can be done only if you do not make a stone image of me. I want you to behave just as you would if I were conversing with you. You would pay attention. Now it borders on worship. This rigidity must go and you will have better results. It takes time, but it is worth attempting."

§

I had a visit from the headmaster at an unusual hour one night. I was in bed. My child had just gone to sleep. And I was preparing to sit up and attempt my daily experiment. I was about to put out the light, when there was a call for me at the gate, "Krishnan, Krishnan." I didn't like to be disturbed. So I kept quiet for a moment hoping that the caller might go away and I regretted I had not put out the light a minute earlier. But the call was repeated. I had to get up and go to the gate. There I saw the headmaster. "Krishnan," he cried on seeing me, "forgive my intrusion at this hour. May I come in and talk to you?"

"Yes, yes," I said, opening the gate. We sat down on the veranda steps. A ray of light fell on him from our sleeping room, and I noticed that he looked very agitated. He sat without speaking for a few minutes. A donkey brayed in a neighbouring lane; wind rustled the avenue trees. I waited for him to open his mouth and tell me his business. I felt he might be wanting a loan of money; he must be in terrible straits.

"I want to ask you . . ." he began. It was at this point that the donkey brayed into the night. "It is a good omen they say, the braying of a donkey. So my request is well-timed."

"Go on," I said, wondering how much he was going to want. "Tell me what you want," I said.

"I want you to take charge of my school, and see that it

does not go to ruin," he said. Worry seemed to have done its work on this poor man, I thought. "All right," I said, but added, "but I've my college. . . ."

"I know it," he said. "But do you think you are happy in your work there?" he asked. I did not reply. It needed no reply. "But who cares for happiness in work? One works for the money . . ." said I in my sober cynicism.

"True, true," he said. "I cannot compel you. Please at least keep an eye on the school, and see that these children are not thrown into a hostile world. . . ."

"All right, all right," I said, not wishing to offend a man mentally unsound. The light from our bedroom illuminated a part of his face. I looked at it. He had the abstraction of a mystic rather than of a maniac. I could not contain myself any longer. And so I cried, "Tell me, what is the matter?" He smiled and said: "This is perhaps my last day. To-morrow, I may be no more." His voice fluttered. "You may remember that I had an astrologer's report with me, and I have also mentioned that my wife would get a big surprise in life; this is it. I never wanted to speak to anyone about it. But I felt I owed it to the children, not to leave the school without any arrangement for it. I hesitated the whole day, and a dozen times came up to your gate and turned away. . . ." I looked at him greatly puzzled: the man was talking as if he were moving to the next street. . . . This was too disturbing—even for me who had been educated to accept and accommodate the idea of death. He spoke on quietly: "My astrologer has written a month-to-month report, and my life has been going on in its details like a time-table. I see it so clearly that nothing ever worries me. I give things just their value—never unduly disturb my mind over affairs; which include also my wife, who, I find, conducts herself according to the time-table." "What is to happen to her?" I asked, almost involuntarily.

"God knows. I only hope she won't start a litigation against my brother, over their house and property." I sat up, thinking it over. It seemed absurd to be talking thus. "No, no, no," I cried. "It can't be."

"It is," he persisted.

"Astrologers are not allowed to mention these things. . . ."

"Not my astrologer. He is not a professional predictor, but a hermit, who can see past, present, and future as one, and give everything its true value. He doesn't want you to put your head under the sand, thinking that you are unseen. Man must essentially be a creature of strength and truth. You would love him if you met him, but I don't know where he is. He came one day for alms, took a fancy to me, and sat down and dictated my life to me after a glance at my palm, and took the road again in the evening. I have never seen him since. But the few hours he was with me he charged my mind with new visions, ideas and strength. My life underwent a revolution. It was after that I left my family and home and set up the school. They jeered at us and made fun of me, but I don't mind. My life has gone on precisely as he predicted."

"You have a duty to your wife and children," I persisted.

"Yes, but what can I do? I shall bequeath to them the school, but would she care for it? Not she."

"What can she do with the school? Will it give her food and shelter?"

"It ought to mean more than that if she had trained herself to view things properly," he replied. "I could have done so much more, if she had taken an interest. But she wouldn't even send the children. So independent a person as that, I believe, will get on whatever may happen." I felt he could not be made to see my point, however much I might argue about it. "Don't bother about it all," he added. "Leave us alone. Will you look after the school? See that it goes on at least till the present set of children leave there? Please promise."

"I will do my best, but I have to mind my college," I added again.

"I think my time is nearing. It is midnight, isn't it? I may not see the sunrise to-morrow." I was greatly moved to hear him say it. I implored him: "Don't believe all this, my friend. You will be back in the morning. Or will you sleep here in my house?" I suggested apprehensively. He shook his head: "It's my last night. I should like to spend it with my wife and children."

"Shall I see you home?" I asked, hoping he wouldn't agree. I had forgotten the child when I made the offer. He brushed it aside: "No, don't trouble yourself. I can go home quite safely. I am quite sober and sound in mind, I assure you. If you have still any doubt about me, see this paper. . . ." He took out of his pocket a folded piece of paper, and spread it out on his knee. He tilted it towards the light, "Go on, read it. I took it out of the file. It is nearly the last sheet, you know," he said with a forced laugh. "Go on, read it aloud." I read out with difficulty: "This person's earthly duties over, he will pass over on this day, surrounded by his wife and children at his last moment. . . ." I read it, and did not know what to say about it. What does one say on such occasions?

"You are looking quite well?" I said testingly.

"I'm in perfect condition," he said. "But what is there to prevent anyone dying in perfect health as well as in ill-health?" he said. This was the strangest man I had ever come across. I had never known this side of the man. I felt foolish and fatuous. I had never thought that he viewed death in this manner, even theoretically. On the one or two occasions he had condoled with me on the loss of my wife, he was casual and off-hand; but I put it down to the delicacy which he might have felt. I never discussed with him my psychic efforts or experiences, thinking that it would not interest him; but now I felt like telling him about them and said: "Do you know, I don't believe in death myself. My wife has communicated with me so often, and has given me directions for self-development." I went on and on. He listened in silence, his head looking large in a shadow on the ground in front of us. He answered: "Don't mistake me. It is all a matter of personal faith and conviction. But I am not interested in the life after death. I have no opinion either way. There may be a continuation in other spheres, under other conditions, or there may not be. It is immaterial to me. The only reality I recognize is death. To me it is nothing more than a full-stop. I have trained myself to view it with calm. Beyond it . . ." he shook his head. "In fact in my prediction, if you will turn over the page, he says something about my next birth too. I'm to be born in a Cochin village to Brahmin parents and so on . . . but I don't really care for that part. . . ."

"When you trust so much in these predictions, you must trust in that too. . . ."

"But my trust is only in regard to matters of this life, not an inch beyond. . . . I've never looked at that page more than once. My knowledge of past, present and future, strictly pertain to this life. Beyond that I have nothing to say, because I believe I shall once again be resolved into the five elements of which I'm composed: and my intelligence and memory may not be more than what we see in air and water!"

I felt very unhappy to hear all this. I thought of my wife —all that I heard from her. Were they all self-deceptions? Was she nothing more than the mute elements, the funeral fire resolving her into vapour, unseen air, and dust? I felt sad and shaken. He said: "This is my view. But don't let it disturb you. . . ." My daughter stirred in her sleep and moaned. I started up. He rose, gripped my hand, and said: "Good-bye. If we meet once again to-morrow, don't laugh at me." "Oh, no," I said. "I shall celebrate it with a feast. I shall think you have a new life."

I saw him off at the gate. He went away without turning his head.

I awoke earlier than usual. I was very anxious about my friend. My child was still asleep. I had a wash, drank my coffee, requested the old lady to mind the child, and went out.

At Anderson Lane my heart thumped with excitement. I gazed towards the headmaster's house. It was still half dark. A few artisans were moving about, and a few more were sleeping in front of their houses. Even this street looked soft in the morning light.

In a dozen bounds I reached the headmaster's house. The door was shut. I strained my ears to catch any sound of weeping inside. But I·heard nothing except the clanging of vessels. The housewife was apparently up, and nothing untoward had happened. I took this as an encouraging sign and decided to turn back. But I changed my mind. I couldn't resist the desire to go in and see. Only the sight of him safe and talking to me would satisfy me. I knocked. His wife opened the door, and scowled on seeing me.

"What do you want?" she asked.

"Is the headmaster in?"

"No."

"Where is he?"

"He doesn't tell me," she said. "Does he keep all those courtesies? Not he. He went out after dinner, and has not been in since. . . . Not for him such things as wife, children, home, and so on. These boys are fatherless . . ." she said bitterly. I was irritated to see her in this mood, so early in the morning. I felt an admiration for the man who had stood her company for so many years. She turned to go. I felt like wringing her neck—it seemed to offer an ideal grip with her hair knotted high up. "Why do men marry such wives?" I reflected. "A moment, lady," I said. "There is a very important thing I want to tell you. Was he not here last night?"

"No. I have told you that," she replied.

"Perhaps you will never see him again, I hope it pleases

you," I said. She could not make out what I meant. She turned, threw at me a puzzled look, and asked, with her throat going dry: "Why?"

"Do you care enough to know?" I asked. "It was in your hands to have made his life happier, while he lived. But now he is gone, and I hope you have a free and happy life before you now. . . ." She let out a shrill cry and cried, "What has happened? What has happened?" By this time her children, dishevelled and in rags as usual, more so because just out of bed, came up rubbing their eyes and stood beside their mother. She embraced them sentimentally and sobbed. "Oh, these are orphans to-day, who will feed them? They are in the streets, from this moment." She wrung her hands and cried, "Tell me sir, tell me, what is happening?" I told her of the prediction and his visit. "Ah, couldn't he have confided this in me, his wife?" She broke down utterly. She collapsed on the floor and her lamentation filled the whole street, and the whole street crowded into the house. I slipped out. I began to wonder what had happened to him. I walked back home, and then saw that my child was still sleeping. My purpose was to search for him by the river, and then tell the police. I stepped out of my house and was going down the road. As I passed the school I saw him standing at the school gate. "Ghost, ghost," I muttered to myself. "I never heard of a ghost being seen by morning light. . . ." He grinned, came towards me, and shook my hands. "I'm not my ghost, be assured," he said. An unusual cheerfulness had seized him. He looked rejuvenated. "Don't look so full of questions. I can't answer them any more than you can. It simply didn't happen, that is all. . . . I don't know why that *Sadhu* thought fit to put my last date thus. One mistake in an otherwise perfect prediction. The first error in it, and the most agreeable. . . ."

"Didn't I say that it might be wrong? . . ." I gripped his hand and jumped about in glee. "I am so happy. . . ."

"So am I," he said. "You have no idea how it has been weighing me down all these years, in spite of what I might have felt and said; it was like having cancer and knowing fully when you would be finished. It was a terrible agony stretching over years. I rejoice it is over. I have no more pages to watch in my notebook. I can live free and happy."

"But there is that thing about your next birth. . . ."

"Rubbish, I don't care. This life is good enough for me. . . ."

"You shouldn't have put such faith in that thing. . . . They are after all . . ."

"But see here, my friend. For all these years it has been so accurate that I'd no reason to doubt its soundness; but this is the first mistake, and the last you know, for the reading stops with this, except for the next birth. I don't know what made that great hermit say this. It might be after all a test," he said. He sighed: "I don't know where he is. No chance of ever clearing this point with his help. . . ." He looked radiant.

"Didn't you go home last night?" I asked.

"No. I went up to my door, and turned back. If I had to die, I'd prefer to wait for it at the school, rather than at home."

"But you said you wished to be with your wife and children."

"Yes. But I felt they did not deserve it on second thoughts."

"Go home, go home," I said. "The whole street is in your house. Poor lady! Her lamentations can be heard over the whole town!"

"Oh, is that so!" he cried in joy. "What a happy piece of information! I don't care. Let her cry till she brings down the sky. I am going to treat myself as dead and my life as a new birth. You will see—I don't know if that hermit might not have meant my death, after all, in that sense. . . ." I implored him to go and relieve his wife and end the confusion in his street.

"Not I," he said. "I'm dead, I wish I could change my face somehow, so that I should not be recognized. . . ."

"Even by your school children?" I asked.

"Oh, no," he said. I tried to hustle him into returning home. But he stubbornly refused. "I have ceased to be my old self, and so don't belong to that home in Anderson Street. . . . It is all over. This school is my house hereafter. I will settle here. . . ."

"But what about them? . . ."

"They can come and see me here if they like, that is all. I will give them a monthly allowance for their upkeep. That is all I am prepared to do, but not behave as a father and a husband hereafter. I didn't sleep a wink the whole night. It is a novel feeling sitting up and waiting for death. . . . I was wondering how it'd take me. I felt so fit and well. When I felt a little drowsy with sleep, I thought the end had come!"

After all I persuaded him to pay a visit (at least the last one) to his house. He agreed, adding: "After all it is not given to every man to watch his own death scene. . . ." We walked there together. People in the street looked at him in wonder and cried: "Here he is." "Yes," he said. "What of it?" Soon the news spread, and a great crowd poured out of his house and surged towards us. The whole of Anderson Street was there—very few tinsmiths were at their foundry, very few blacksmiths and tailors at their work. People surrounded and fired questions at him. But he refused to answer anyone. "I can't tell you why I am alive," he said. "There is no explanation for it, as there is no explanation for death." The crowd gaped at him and pressed us on all sides. "I never imagined that I had such a large public!" he said. "I thought I was fairly obscure!"

His wife, whom news of his arrival reached, picked herself up, her hair all over her face, swollen and tear-drenched. She looked at him, and let out a cry of relief: "Oh, my lord, you are here! What demon thought fit to tell me . . .?" She fell down and clung to his feet. His children came up and, with cries of rapture, hung on to his arms. He tried to shake himself free, but found it difficult. The crowd looked at him expectantly. He faced them and said: "Why don't you all go away now?" They murmured something and waited for an explanation. He looked at them helplessly, with his family clinging to his feet. The crowd looked at him. He put his hand into his pocket, and took out the slip of paper, jerked it open and held it to the crowd. "Who can read this?" A man came forward, received the slip and read it. "Read it aloud," the headmaster commanded; at which he read out the prophesy to the gathering, and the headmaster added, "This is the prediction and it has not proved false. I tell you, friends, no more of this wife and family for me. You may treat me as dead or as one who has taken *Sanyasa Ashrama.*"

His wife protested and cried hoarsely. But he was adamant. He announced his decision grandly. "She will get her money for her monthly expenses, but that is all. They will never see me here again. . . ." She clung to him and pleaded: "Whatever wrong I have committed forgive me. I will be careful hereafter. . . ." He shook her off without a word. The children came after him. "You may all come and see me in school later. But remember you have no father any more. . . ." He pushed his way through the crowd, and walked away. I followed him sheepishly. The whole business was too confusing. I didn't know what to make of it. His wife ran after us and appealed to me. I looked at her helplessly. I felt a tremendous pity for this creature now. I said: "Headmaster, just think . . ."

"Krishnan, leave me alone," he said. "I have a far greater work to do, and I'm going to do it. I feel such a freedom now. . . ." He set his face and walked off resolutely. The crowd followed us for a while, and then dissipated. His wife and children followed, "Go back," he said, "create a scene if you like, it is none of my business to stop you, but don't put me in that scene, that is all, do you understand?"

Months rolled on. Life falls into ruts of routine, one day following another, expended in set activities: child, school, college, boys, walk, and self-development. This last was the most enchanting item of my life's programme. It was a perpetual excitement, ever promising some new riches in the realm of experience and understanding. I sat up at nights faithfully following the instructions she had given, keeping my mind open, and I was beginning to be aware of a slight improvement in my sensibilities. There was a real cheerfulness growing within me, memory hurt less, and I was more and more aware of vague perceptions, like a three-quarter deaf man catching the rustle of a dress of someone he loves. . . . That this was not a vain presumption on my part was borne out at a sitting we had about this time. Our regular Wednesday meetings were gradually given up, and we met now at unspecified intervals, once in six or seven weeks or so. Nor did I feel these days the hopeless longing for a regular sitting. My nightly contacts gave me peace. "At first it will be a matter of belief," I remember her saying. I clung to it fast; "Belief, belief." Above reason, scepticism, and even immediate failures, I clung to it. "I do meet her when I sit down, and she is with me when I sit with my mind passive, calling her," I repeated to myself night and day, and it wrought a curious success. Any other thought was impossible.

After a long time my friend gave me a sitting one dusk beside the lotus pond. The hour was as beautiful as ever. She started by saying: "Have you observed one effect of your development? I can say now that you are developing quite satisfactorily. Think of about four days ago—the small hours of the night. I tried to appear and make my presence felt by you. I purposely wore the garb, which you called on a former occasion, 'gorgeous'—the blue, shimmering with light interwoven. I appeared, and I tried to make my presence felt. We went out together into the garden.

We walked for a while, indeed for a considerable time, and then the experience ended. You returned to bed, and went to sleep again. . . . You turned over and resumed your sleep, thinking that you had had a slight disturbance. If there is any chance that you remember this experience, let me assure you that it was I myself who was there with you and if you remember it, it is a sign that you are developing quite well. . . ."

It required no great effort to recollect this. I was over come with great joy. I seized my friend's hand and cried "It is true, absolutely true. I thought it was a private dream. It wasn't. How little do we know what a dream is, how little do we understand! Yes, friend, every word of it is true. I don't remember it clearly, but I dreamt of her as standing before me with some gorgeous dress on. I greeted her, and I held her hand. We went out into the garden. That is all the dream I remember. It was not a shadow cast and created by a troubled mind, but the substance. . . . It was she, it was herself," I cried.

"Ask her," I said. "After the dream we parted. How long did she stay with me? How often does she meet me?" It was a series of incoherent questions. I myself had no clear notion what I wanted to ask or how to ask it. I only felt the urge to ask questions. . . . She evidently understood whatever it was that was in my mind, and replied: "I shall try to answer these questions of yours, but I have to do it unsatisfactorily, because of their nature. You have been in this garden house to-day for over two hours. Can you say you have been in the company of your friend just once, twice or thrice? The moment you call someone who is in the next room, he answers you and comes to your side if need be. I am present at your side when you sit for development and communion. At other times it is as if I were in the next room, aware of the fact of your presence, easily accessible and ready to come at your slightest behest. You may even think of the walls separating us as walls of glass."

It was a delightful surprise for me one day, returning home from college, to receive a card from my mother, saying she was coming by the eleven o'clock bus on the following morning. I told the child immediately. But she asked: "Who is coming with her? Is she bringing dolls?"

"Oh, yes, yes," I said. I cancelled the walk that evening. The house needed a lot of tidying up, otherwise mother would spend her entire stay doing it. I took off my shirt, tucked up my *dhoti*, and wrapped a towel round my head, as a preparation. In the kitchen I told the old lady, "Please polish all the vessels. My mother will be here to-morrow. You know how she views these things!" The old lady pulled down all the vessels, and the purr of her broom, sweeping the store, resounded through the house. I took a duster and a long-handled broom, and cleaned up the cornices and dusted everything, dragged the trunks about, pulled down all the books, sneezed and caught a cold which lasted a day or two. The child followed me about. She had caught the fever of activity and followed me about whining and imploring for work. I said: "Your toy box, you have stuffed it in such a way that we cannot close it. It looks ugly in the hall with its lid thrown back agape; do something about it. Throw away all the unimportant things, and clean and arrange the things in the box. What will your grandmother say if she sees your box?"

Leela at first grumbled and demanded to be alloted some worth-while work. But I persuaded her by dinning into her over and over again: "What will your grandmother say if she sees your box!" Finally she realized the seriousness of the position and said: "Yes." She went over to her box, and as usual held it by the handle on one side and tipped the entire contents on the floor. They came down with a terrific clatter and crash—a dozen cardboard boxes, her slate, books, wooden toys and engines and motors and dolls, all crashed down in a heap on the floor. She squatted in their midst and said, "Shall I throw away the things I don't want?"

"Yes." She started this operation. She picked up and looked at each, and said: "This thing is not wanted" and flung it off to another corner of the hall. This mood had caught her and cardboard boxes and all kinds of things which she cherished seemed to vex her suddenly by their very presence. In a short time in another corner of the hall were heaped the bulk of her possessions. Except her school books and five wooden vessels, and a large doll, all the other things were there. I had to go on with my work in another part of the house. But when I saw what she had done, I protested. "I tidied up this hall." "I will throw them in the street now," she explained. She came over, picked up a handful, took them to the street, returned with the handful, looked wistfully at the heap and appealed: "Father, I must put them all back in the box."

"Why?"

"They are all important . . ." she said very earnestly, looking at me fixedly. And forthwith all the toys returned to the box in the same manner as they came out—in a clattering rush.

I applied for leave in order to meet my mother. I waited at the bus stand, beyond the market square. The glare was blinding; the dust unbearable. The bus from Trichinopoly due to arrive at eleven was not showing any signs even half an hour later. I was growing impatient. The bus service people had made no provision for waiting. There was a miserable tamarind tree with sparse leaves, under which were gathered three women waiting to catch the bus, a cooly waiting for fares, an ass in the neighbourhood who could not stand the heat of the day—and a *jutka* with horse strapped to it; the *jutka* man had just brought it in so that there should be a patch of shade on the horse's snout; he seemed to feel satisfied that he had saved the horse from the heat of the sun. The *jutka* man was also waiting for the bus to arrive and provide him a fare. He waited for the bus, felt drowsy, curled up in his seat and was soon asleep. The donkey moved nearer and put his mouth into the bunch of grass thrown down on the ground for the horse to munch while the master slept. The donkey pulled out a mouthful, at which the horse stamped and neighed. The cart driver woke up and flourished his whip at the donkey. And we enjoyed the whole show, although the sun baked us.

After all the bus arrived at twelve precisely. Parched and dusty, my mother wriggled herself out from among her fellow passengers. "How is the child?" she asked getting down. It was her very first question. We put her luggage into the *jutka*, haggled with the driver, and started home. Over the rattling of the wheels she spoke—complaining about my correspondence, enquiring about the child, if the old cook was well, and how I was managing to look after the child. I was tremendously pleased: as I looked at her, warm, and throbbing with life and enquiries, it seemed to restore for a moment one's sense of security, the solid factors of life, and its warmth and interests.

My child as usual was waiting at the door, and hardly had the old lady got down from the carriage when she ran to her and was, in a moment, in her arms. I could hardly comprehend—there were so many excited changes between the grandmother and daughter. "Granny, open your trunk, open your trunk, what have you brought for me? . . ." She went on pestering even before the trunk and bed were brought in. They went in. I paid off the carriage, received the change, and followed. By that time I found there was a great argument going on between them—the little one standing on my mother's ancient trunk, and insisting upon having it opened immediately. My mother, mildly protesting, requesting to be allowed to rest for a few minutes: "Oh, child, there're no shops in our little place. What should I bring you?" There were tears in her eyes. She cast a slight look at the room on our right in the hall, my wife's room, now

(197)

empty, and touched away the tears with the tip of her fingers.

My daughter stamped on the steel trunk, and made such a row that I felt it was time for me to interfere: "H'sh, you must learn . . ." I began. But my mother stopped: "Don't be harsh; poor child, jump down, I'll open the trunk for you." She muttered as she fumbled with the key and the lock: "You used to be exactly the same: you'd cling to your father, and wouldn't let him remove even his sandals before giving you your presents." She opened the trunk. My daughter sat on her lap and gazed into the trunk expectantly. My mother pulled out a few sarees, a couple of towels, jackets, a horn comb, and lastly a little casket, out of which she produced a gold chain. "I had this made for the child at the town shop when your father went there last time. He is the only goldsmith we have near at hand, though fifteen miles away. . . ." She slipped the chain over the child's head. "Three sovereigns weight. How do you like it?" Leela looked down at her chest with great satisfaction. The gold chain glistened, but I was absorbed elsewhere. I was staring at the casket from which mother had taken out the chain. "Mother, give it here!" I cried.

I examined it, measured it with my finger, held it off and scrutinized it—an ivory-worked sandalwood casket. "Wait a minute!" I said and ran into my room. I pulled out the table-drawer, turned over the pages containing my wife's messages. She had written: "It is not a very big box—about eight or ten inches long, three inches high, and about four inches wide . . . the lid of the box is not flat but slightly elevated. . . . It was given to me by my mother-in-law. Box of ivory and sandalwood. . . ." I took out a little scale and measured the box. The measurements she had given were slightly more or less by about half an inch all round. I put away the scale and read over the message again. I couldn't yet decide whether her reference was to this casket or some other. And presently I came upon a sentence, which had nearly escaped me all these days. "The casket is mounted on short ivory legs, resembling tiger-paws." I lifted the casket and examined its legs. The tiger-paws were there. I grew red with excitement. I clutched the pages and was about to run out to read them to my mother. But I checked myself. I'd never spoken of these to anyone so far. She might not see it as I did, she might doubt, cross-examine, feel on the whole disturbed. It meant a new habit of thinking in regard to death, all too difficult at her age, or she might think I was mad. In any case this information was too precious to part with, to make public even to a mother. I put the papers into the drawer, went back, and sat down beside my mother. I said, "I like this box, mother, what do you keep in it?" "All your," she lowered her voice and muttered in my ear, so that the child should not hear, "wife's jewels. I got this from my sister years ago. Susila used to be fond of it and had once or twice even made bold to ask for it. But somehow I didn't give it to her. . . . Now I keep her jewels in it. I'll give it to the child. . . ."

"Can I keep it with me?" I asked.

"Why do you want it? It's a jewel box. . . ."

"I like it, mother. I'll keep some of the child's knick-knacks in it," I said. She gave it to me.

This discovery made me write to my father-in-law next day for the bundle of fourteen letters, which Susila had often mentioned. Four days later I received a reply. "I have searched every nook and corner in the house and every box, but not a single letter is to be found. Perhaps they were in that lot which I saw her and her brother destroying in the fire one day when she was here last. I hope you will forgive this disappointment and not feel dejected." In his last paragraph he wrote: "I don't know if you are already aware of it. I have written to your father about it. I intend to make an endowment for my dear grandchild Leela to benefit her when she comes of a marriageable age."

I went to my mother. She was sitting in the hall, combing

(199)

the child's hair. She did everything with her own hands nowadays, often complaining that my neglect had made the child's tresses shorter.

"I've a letter from my father-in-law," I began.

"Oh, has he written to you about this matter?" she said slyly pointing at the child.

"Yes—he has."

"He wrote to your father," she said. "He proposes to set apart," she indicated with her fingers six, "for this person, to be given to her on the day of her marriage."

"Whose marriage, mother?" the child asked.

"Somebody's marriage, child, don't listen to our talk," she said, and continued. "And your father also proposes to set apart a similar sum for the same purpose."

"Oh," I said, not knowing what to say. "She is very lucky!"

My mother smiled cynically, "Of course you must admire her luck." She added, with a sigh! "What are these? Can these things ever compensate for the absence of that one person?"

"Who is to be married, mother?" the child asked again.

"A girl in our place," said her grandmother.

"How big is she?" asked the child. For some unknown reason she seemed to be concerned with the bulk of this bride. My mother said: "Even if she has proved unlucky in other matters, let her at least have a well-provided future."

My mother stayed with us for four weeks. My father's condition had improved and she could stay with us—happy days; the child bloomed with a new life, under her handling. She ceased to approach me for company or help. She stuck to her grandmother morning to night and slept on her bed at night. She bloomed in this warmth. Children need above all else the warmth of a mother's touch. Watching her now I realized with a pang that the very best I could provide was still hopelessly inadequate. And if the child had looked happy under my handling it was more out of tolerance than anything else.

On the eve of her departure mother was packing up. The child stood beside her watching and asked: "Mother, are you going?"

"Yes, dear, yes."

"Don't go," she said and looked so miserable that mother said: "Will you come with me?" Leela jumped at this suggestion. She cried: "Give me a box, father, I want to put my things into it." I said soothingly: "There is time, there is time." At which she became uncontrollable. My mother said: "Seriously, why don't you let me take her with me?" I said: "She will not go. She will want me too. . . ." Granny said: "Your father will not come with us."

"Oh!" said the child, "why not?"

"He has his school to attend. . . ."

"But I have also my school," Leela replied irrelevantly.

"So, you must stay and let grandmother go," I said.

"Why will she not stay here?" the child asked. I saw that she had made up her mind to go with her grandmother. She was thrilled to hear that there were other children in the house. My sister's two children and a few others, numbering in all seven. Leela could not understand what it meant. How could there be children at home? Children were to be seen only in schools. So she asked: "Is it a school?"

Next afternoon she was ready to start with her grandmother. I felt acute anxiety about sending her by bus. I had never been separated from her; the thought appalled me. But as I saw her bubbling over with enthusiasm I told myself: "Don't be selfish. She must have her own life." Her trunk of toys and her bed of clothes were there, perched upon the bus next afternoon. I had been dinning into my mother's ears instructions regarding the child. Even as the conductor blew his whistle I shouted instructions. "Don't allow her to lean out. See that she doesn't eat too many sweets. She gets a racking cough at nights. Oil and bath every Friday, but the water must not be too hot. . . . She must be immediately wrapped up. . . . Milk, only half a tumbler. . . ." My mother merely smiled.

The child said: "Father, I will write you a letter."

The bus groaned and moved, and was soon lost in a screen of dust of its own kicking.

§

A few weeks later a letter arrived from my father, enclosing a scrap of paper with a scrawl on it. My father wrote: "The enclosed letter is from your Leela. I just mentioned to-day that I was going to write to you, and at once she declared she had much to write to you too. I gave her my pencil and the paper, and she has written this letter." I looked at a small slip of paper: the familiar memo pad of my father's neatly torn in half. I saw huge scrawls looking like trees or clouds and a few letters of the alphabet and at the bottom the huge word: LEELA. It was folded and on the flap was written "To my beloved father", which was in my father's handwriting, though he tried to disguise it by writing rounded capital letters. Moreover there was his favourite ink. I looked at this communication from my daughter and felt very happy. I folded it and put it in my purse as if it were a rare document. My father's letter explained: "You may want to know what she has written. Here is the paraphrase. She is always surrounded by a dozen children, always playing, building a castle on the pyol on which her grandfather is resting. He is spending all his time watching her and what a great joy it is. It has made him forget his illness, watching her. In the evening she goes out with her granny to the tank or the garden. She is in splendid health, eating and digesting everything that her granny gives her. A teacher comes to teach her in the afternoon. She sleeps beside her granny. I asked her if she wants her father. "Yes," she says, "let him come here," which is a very profound suggestion. I would ask you to come and spend your week-end holidays with her. After all she is only four hours off from your place. So I hope you will not allow any feeling of loneliness to oppress you. . . ."

I boarded the bus for the village next week-end.

§

I returned from the village. The house seemed unbearably dull. But I bore it. "There is no escape from loneliness and separation . . ." I told myself often. "Wife, child, brothers, parents, friends. . . . We come together only to go apart again. It is one continuous movement. They move away from us as we move away from them. The law of life can't be avoided. The law comes into operation the moment we detach ourselves from our mother's womb. All struggle and misery in life is due to our attempt to arrest this law or get away from it or in allowing ourselves to be hurt by it. The fact must be recognized. A profound unmitigated loneliness is the only truth of life. All else is false. My mother got away from her parents, my sisters from our house, I and my brother away from each other, my wife was torn away from me, my daughter is going away with my mother, my father has gone away from his father, my earliest friends—where are they? They scatter apart like the droplets of a waterspray. The law of life. No sense in battling against it. . . ." Thus I reconciled myself to this separation with less struggle than before. I read a lot, I wrote a lot, I reflected as much as I could. I saw pictures, went out for walks, and frequently met my friend the headmaster. I spent a great deal of my time watching the children at play or hearing him narrate his stories for the children as they sat under the mango tree in the school compound. When I sat there at the threshold of his hut and watched the children, all sense of loneliness ceased to oppress, and I felt a deep joy and contentment stirring within me. I felt there was nothing more for me to demand of life. The headmaster's presence was always most soothing. He was a very happy man nowadays. His school had over two hundred pupils studying in it and he was able to spend as much as he wanted in staffing and equipping the school.

His wife and children visited him often, at least thrice in a day. He treated them kindly, although he still refused to visit them at home, and strictly forbade them to call him father or husband. His wife, a greatly chastened person now, often implored him to let her bring him his food. He firmly declined the offer, declaring: "No, it is there that all the trouble starts. The kitchen is the deadliest arsenal a woman possesses."

◆

CHAPTER EIGHT

My mind was made up. I was in search of a harmonious existence and everything that disturbed that harmony was to be rigorously excluded, even my college work. One whole night I sat up in the loneliness of my house thinking it over, and before the night was out my mind was made up. I could not go on with that work; nor did I need the one hundred rupees they gave me. At first I had thought of sending in my resignation by letter to Brown, and making an end of it. I would avoid all the personal contacts, persuasions, and all the possible sentimentalities inevitable in the act of snapping familiar roots. I would send in a letter which would be a classic in its own way, and which would singe the fingers of whoever touched it. In it I was going to attack a whole century of false education. I was going to explain why I could no longer stuff Shakespeare and Elizabethan metre and Romantic poetry for the hundredth time into young minds and feed them on the dead mutton of literary analysis and theories and histories, while what they needed was lessons in the fullest use of the mind. This education had reduced us to a nation of morons; we were strangers to our own culture and camp followers of another culture, feeding on leavings and garbage.

After coffee I sat down at my table with several sheets of large paper before me. I began "Dear Mr. Brown: This is my letter of resignation. You will doubtless want to know the reasons. Here they are. . . ." I didn't like this. It was too breezy. I scored it out and began again. I filled three sheets,

and reading it over, felt ashamed of myself. It was too the-
atrical and pompous for my taste. I was entangled too much
in theories and platitudes and holding forth to all whom it
might concern. It was like a rabid attack on all English
writers, which was hardly my purpose. "What fool could be
insensible to Shakespeare's sonnets or the *Ode to the West
Wind* or 'A thing of beauty is a joy for ever'?" I reflected.
"But what about examinations and critical notes? Didn't
these largely take the place of literature? What about our
own roots?" I thought over it deeply and felt very puzzled.
I added: "I am up against the system, the whole method and
approach of a system of education which makes us morons,
cultural morons, but efficient clerks for all your business and
administrative offices. You must not think that I am opposed
to my particular studies of authors. . . ." The repetition of
ideas uttered a hundred times before. It looked like a rehash
of an article entitled "Problems of High Education", which
appeared again and again in a week-end educational supple-
ment—the yarn some "educationist" was spinning out for
ten rupees a column.

"This is not what I want to say," I muttered to myself
and tore up the letter and stuffed it into the wastepaper
basket. "There is something far deeper that I wish to say."

I took out a small sheet of paper and wrote: "Dear Sir, I
beg to tender my resignation for personal reasons. I request
you to relieve me immediately. . . ." I put it in an envelope.

§

I walked into Brown's room that afternoon with this envelope in my hand. He was in a leisurely mood sitting back in
his swivel chair, reading a book. I placed the envelope before
him.

"What is this? Applying for leave?" he said, a smile
spreading on his aged handsome face. . . . "Be seated. . . ."
He read the letter. His face turned slightly red. He looked

at me and said: "What is the matter?" He lit a cigarette, blew out a ring of smoke and waited for my answer, looking at me with his greenish eyes. I merely replied: "I can't go on with this work any longer, sir. . . ."

"Any special reason?" I remained silent. I didn't know what to say. I replied: "I am taking up work in a children's school." "Oh!" he said. . . . "But I didn't know you had primary school training. . . ." he replied. I looked at him in despair; his western mind, classifying, labelling, departmentalizing. . . . I merely replied: "I am beginning a new experiment in education, with another friend." 'Oh, that is interesting," he replied. "But look here, must you resign? Couldn't you keep it on as an extra interest. . . . We do want a lot of experimenting in education, but you could always. . ." He went on suggesting it as a hobby. I replied: "Sir, what I am doing in the college hardly seems to me work. I mug up and repeat and they mug up and repeat in examinations. . . . This hardly seems to me work, Mr. Brown. It is a fraud I am practising for a consideration of a hundred rupees a month. . . . It doesn't please my innermost self. . . ." Thus I rambled on.

"I do not know," he said scratching his head. "It seems to me unfortunate. However, I wouldn't make up my mind in a hurry if I were you. . . ."

"I have thought it over deeply, sir." I replied, "My mind is made up."

He asked: "What does it mean to you financially?"

"About twenty-five rupees a month. . . ." I replied.

"That means a cutting down. . . ."

"That is so. I have no use for money. I have no family. My child is being looked after by others and they have provided for her future too. I have a few savings. I have no use for a hundred rupees a month. . . ." Brown looked quite baffled. I added: "Of all persons on earth, I can afford to do what seems to me work, something which satisfies my innermost aspiration. I will write poetry and live and work with children and watch their minds unfold. . . ."

"Quite," he replied. "A man like you ought to derive equal delight in teaching literature. You have done admirably as a teacher of literature. . . ."

I shook my head. "I don't feel I have done anything of the kind. . . ."

"Do you mean to say that all those poets and dramatists have meant nothing to you?"

I was in danger of repeating the letter I had torn up. "It is not that. I revere them. And I hope to give them to these children for their delight and enlightenment, but in a different measure and in a different manner." I rambled on thus. I could not speak clearly. Brown bore with me patiently. Our interview lasted an hour. At the end of it he said: "Take another week, if you like, to consider. I do wish you wouldn't leave us." He held out his hand. I gripped his large warm palm, and walked out of the room.

§

They arranged a grand send-off for me. The function was timed to begin at six. I arrived five minutes earlier and was at once seized on by Sastri and Rangappa, the moving spirits of the occasion. They waited at the porch and the moment they sighted me, they dashed forward, and gripped my hand and dragged me on to the quadrangle, where they had made spectacular arrangements. The hotel man had risen to the occasion; he had tied up coloured buntings and streamers, spread his embroidered table-cloth on a dozen tables, and placed his usual gold mohur bunches on nickel vases. Porcelain cups and plates clanked somewhere. White-shirted serving boys stood respectfully on the edge of the scene. They looked at me with respectful interest. In fact everyone looked on me as a sort of awe-inspiring personality. What was there in this to make a sudden hero of me? It was very embarrassing. On the air was borne a gentle suggestion of

(208)

jasmine and rose. I knew a garland was waiting for me some-where.

I was pressed into a high-backed chair. Next to mine was another chair for Brown. On my left sat Gajapathy. All around were gathered a miscellaneous crowd of teachers and boys. Everybody kept staring at me. I felt very unhappy. I had never felt more selfconscious in all my life. Gajapathy was highly nervous and excited, and wriggled in his chair. He kept muttering "Why is not Brown here yet?" And con-stantly looked at his watch.

There was the sound of a car stopping outside. "The Principal," everyone muttered. The creaking of fast foot-steps and Brown arrived in an evening suit. "Even he is dressed for the occasion," I said to myself. "Why, why all this ceremony?" Gajapathy shot up in his seat. Sastri and Rangappa went forward to receive him.

Now we were all ready. Brown bent over to me and whis-pered: "I was afraid the weather wouldn't let us use the quadrangle to-day." I looked at the sky and mumbled some-thing about the weather. Gajapathy, uninvited, joined us in this conversation. "Rain is very unusual at this season, but strangely enough we have had it for the past two days. But to-day our luck is good. . . ."

"Yes," Brown echoed, "rather unusual. . . ." Perspiring and puffing, Rangappa moved about, and passed a signal on to the servers. There were nearly ten courses. Brown lightly touched each one of them; withdrew with quick caution from items which were over-spiced (experience born of thirty years' stay in India), put small bits of sweets into his mouth and sent them on without moving his lips. Gajapathy sat back with his fingers locked into each other, sadly looking at the plates. The other guests were talking among themselves, a merry hum pervaded the place. I asked Gajapathy: "Why?" He shook his head sadly: "I am a sick man, can't afford these luxuries. . . ." Brown looked at him without comment. He wanted to change the subject from personal

(209)

ailments. He held up between his thumb and forefinger a gold coloured sweet and said: "This is also a variant of *jilebi*, isn't it?"

"I suppose so, sir," replied Gajapathy. "I think it is the stuff made of American flour, while the real *jilebi* . . ."

"Ah, I'm right. I know my *jilebi* when I see it." A smile spread round his eyes. We laughed. Rangappa, who had been observing us from his chair far off, looked at us enquiringly, and also smiled out of politeness. . . .

When coffee was served, Brown clutched his cup and stood up. A silence fell on the gathering: "To the health of our guest of this evening," he said in his deep sonorous voice. "I don't know if it would be right to toast with coffee but we won't bother about these proprieties now. . . ." On behalf of the assembly he wished me all prosperity and happiness. He continued, "I have known him, I have lost count now how many years. I remember the day he came to my room with application for a seat in English Honours. I've seen him grow under my eyes; he has shown himself an able teacher. The boys have loved him. And I'm sure they have had reason to dread him very much as an examiner." Some boys looked at me with a grin. "Everywhere, under every condition, he has proved himself to be an uncompromising idealist. His constant anxiety has been to find the world good enough for his own principles of life and letters. Few men would have the courage to throw up a lucrative income and adopt one very much lower. But he has done it. Success must be measured by its profitlessness, said a French philosopher. Our college can look upon this idealist with justifiable pride. And . . ." looking at me he said: "when your institution has developed and made a mark in the world, I do hope you will allow us a small share of the gratification that you yourself may feel. . . . Gentlemen, I'm sure you will all join me in wishing our friend all success." He raised his cup.

I felt too disturbed to look up. My hands trembled. I sat looking down. Brown sat down. I was too moved: "Many thanks," I murmured. Three more speeches followed: one by Rangappa who traced our friendship to the hostel days, one by Sastri and one by an Honours boy. "Our country needs more men like our beloved teacher who is going out to-day," he said in his high-pitched tender voice. "The national regeneration is in his hands. . . ." Goodwill and adulation enveloped me like thick mist. In the end I got up and said: "Gentlemen, permit me to thank you all for your kind words. Let me assure you I'm retiring, not with a feeling of sacrifice for a national cause, but with a very selfish purpose. I'm seeking a great inner peace. I find I can't attain it unless I withdraw from the adult world and adult work into the world of children. And there, let me assure you, is a vast storehouse of peace and harmony. I have not had in mind anything more than that, and I hope you will correct your estimates accordingly. I am deeply grateful to you and to our chief for your great kindness. . . ." I sat down because I found my voice quivering.

Rangappa brought a heavy rose and jasmine garland and slipped it over my neck. He brought another and put it on the Principal. Applause. "Three cheers for our guest of the evening," somebody screamed. "Hip! Hip . . ." burst like an explosion. And then "Three cheers for our Principal. . . ." On this thunderous note our evening concluded.

§

I was walking down our lone street late at night, enveloped in the fragrance of the jasmine and rose garland, slung on my arm. "For whom am I carrying this jasmine home?" I asked myself. Susila would treasure a garland for two whole days, cutting up and sticking masses of it in her hair morning and evening. "Carrying a garland to a lonely house—a dreadful job," I told myself.

I fumbled with the key in the dark, opened the door and switched on the light. I hung up the garland on a nail and kicked up the roll of bedding. The fragrance permeated the whole house. I sprinkled a little water on the flowers to keep them fresh, put out the light and lay down to sleep.

The garland hung by the nail right over my head. The few drops of water which I sprinkled on the flowers seemed to have quickened in them a new life. Their essences came forth into the dark night as I lay in bed, bringing a new vigour with them. The atmosphere became surcharged with strange spiritual forces. Their delicate aroma filled every particle of the air, and as I let my mind float in the ecstasy, gradually perceptions and senses deepened. Oblivion crept over me like a cloud. The past, present and the future welded into one.

I had been thinking of the day's activities and meetings and associations. But they seemed to have no place now. I checked my mind. Bits of memory came floating—a gesture of Brown's, the toy house in the dentist's front room, Rangappa with a garland, and the ring of many speeches and voices—all this was gently overwhelmed and swept aside, till one's mind became clean and bare and a mere chamber of fragrance. It was a superb, noble intoxication. And I had no choice but to let my mind and memories drown in it. I softly called "Susila! Susila, my wife . . ." with all my being. It sounded as if it were a hypnotic melody. "My wife . . . my wife, my wife. . . ." My mind trembled with this rhythm, I forgot myself and my own existence. I fell into a drowse, whispering, "My wife, wife." How long? How could I say? When I opened my eyes again she was sitting on my bed looking at me with an extraordinary smile in her eyes.

"Susila! Susila!" I cried. "You here!" "Yes, I'm here, have always been here." I sat up leaning on my pillow. "Why do you disturb yourself?" she asked.

"I am making a place for you," I said, edging away a little. I looked her up and down and said: "How well you look!" Her complexion had a golden glow, her eyes sparkled with a new light, her saree shimmered with blue interwoven with "light" as she had termed it. . . . "How beautiful!" I said looking at it. "Yes, I always wear this when I come to you. I know you like it very much," she said. I gazed on her face. There was an overwhelming fragrance of jasmine surrounding her. "Still jasmine-scented!" I commented.

"Oh wait," I said and got up. I picked up the garland from the nail and returned to bed. I held it to her "For you as ever. I somehow feared you wouldn't take it. . . ." She received it with a smile, cut off a piece of it and stuck it in a curve on the back of her head. She turned her head and asked: "Is this all right?"

"Wonderful," I said, smelling it.

A cock crew. The first purple of the dawn came through our window, and faintly touched the walls of our room. "Dawn!" she whispered and rose to her feet.

We stood at the window, gazing on a slender, red streak over the eastern rim of the earth. A cool breeze lapped our faces. The boundaries of our personalities suddenly dissolved. It was a moment of rare, immutable joy—a moment for which one feels grateful to Life and Death.